ISBN 978-0-260-64874-7
PIBN 10961931

Letters from Oberlin Alumni . . .

One of Oberlin's "Lost Sheep" Sends Kindest Regards

Norwich, Vermont
April 5, 1943

Dear Mr. Harris:

Thank you for sending me a copy of your very interesting special newspaper edition of the Oberlin *Alumni Magazine*.

Somewhere back in 1900 I was registered in Oberlin Academy and spent a very pleasant year and a half in that institution. Owing to a Saturday night opening of a new saloon in Elyria, attended by myself and several friends, and complicated by the presence on the returning trolley car of a member of the faculty, my connection with the Academy was terminated with abruptness and finality.

Since that time I do not remember of ever having received any communications from Oberlin until the above noted edition arrived today, and I congratulate you on including one of the lost sheep in your list. As class agent for my Dartmouth class of 1905 I have had several years work as collector of funds for our annual Alumni Campaign. As you no doubt know Dartmouth has a very excellent record in the matter of alumni contributions, the most recent completed fund bringing in nearly $200,000 from 57% of all former students. From graduates the percentage of contributors was 71, from non-graduates the percentage was 25. While it is true that the average gift from graduates is larger than that of non-graduates, the fact remains that the total receipts from non-graduates is a very helpful addition to the total.

I think you are on the right track in circularizing all of your former students and wish you success in the plan. Once you get $5.00 or $10.00 from a non-graduate it is surprising to see how his interest in his old school becomes rejuvenated. From my recollection of the rules and regulations of Oberlin around 1900 it occurs to me that you must have quite an impressive number of students who failed to graduate!

With kindest regards, please believe me,
—C. C. Hills.

Thank you for the newspaper. Let's have more!

—Grace Hageman, '34.

AVIATION CADET JAMES HALL, '42
. . . now in the final weeks of his training as a U. S. Navy dive bomber pilot at Kingsville Texas. Cadet Hall is the son of Professor ('07) and Mrs. James H. Hall (Florence Jenney, '07).

Ex-Review Editor Bill Tucker Counts Our Merits and Demerits

University of Chicago
April 5, 1943

Dear Chuck:

Congratulations on your newspaper edition of The *Alumni Magazine*. It is distinctly a workmanlike job.

Thought I'd take you up on the request in column 1, page 1, for reactions to said issue. Things I like about the issue: the greater space for letters, especially those from men in the services; the report by Treasurer Davis; the bringing up-to-date of the list of men and women in the services; the editorial, "Looking Ahead," by President Wilkins; the article by Dr. Joseph F. King, new pastor of First Church; the brief news items, such as the one about Ivanore Barnes leaving, Rodzinski's farewell concert, the Hemingways, etc.; the Sports Page; and, of course, the news of the classes, which is always interesting.

Specifically, if the reaction you receive encourages and warrants it, I would suggest that in future Newspaper Editions (as they may be planned), various administrative officers of the College be asked to report on various aspects of the work of their departments. Davis' report was a good send-off.

On the debit side of the balance, there is much less to say. I am not particularly interested in Alumni Club news, but that may be just a personal preference. So much display to results of the Alumni Fund drive may be warranted by tactical considerations, but leaves me only mildly interested (after I have sent my check!). There might be more news, personal and otherwise, of the faculty.

One glaring error: on page 9, the paragraph on Mary Ellen Duffey, '44, the new business manager of the *Review*, states she "is believed to be the first woman ever appointed" as business manager. That should have been a statement easily verified by reference to the files of the Review; and in any event your memory should have served you well, for I believe I am correct in stating that a classmate of yours, Emilie Ann Jones, '28, was advertising manager of the *Review* from '26 to '27 (when Wayne DeVyver, '27, was business manager), and she became business manager in the spring of 1927. She was a darned good one, too, as I ought to know, working with her as I did as Editor for a year. Keep up the good work!

—(Dr.) Bill Tucker, '29.

Chuck Giauque and His Two Sons Are All in Uniform

Gentlemen:

I wish to thank you for your kindness in sending me the special issue of The *Oberlin Alumni Magazine*.

I am serving as Physical Training Officer of this Naval Station. One of my sons, "Chuck," is pilot of a Flying Fortress in Europe and has just been decorated for valor. His ship brought down three German planes. A second son, "Hank," is a Cadet Officer of the Merchant Marine and is serving on a ship on the Atlantic.

—"Chuck" Giauque, '16
Lt. Comdr., USNR

(Letters Continued—Inside Back Cover)

The Oberlin Alumni Magazine, April, 1943; Volume 39; Number 6. Published monthly except in January, July, August and September. Published by the Alumni Association of Oberlin College, Inc. Subscription price $3.00 a year. Single copies, 35 cents. Entered as second-class matter October 3, 1904, at the post office, Oberlin, Ohio, under the Act of Congress of March 3, 1879

OBERLIN ALUMNI

APRIL, 1943

MAGAZINE

VOL. 39; NO. 6

CHARLES A. MOSHER, '28
Editor

THOMAS E. HARRIS, '33
General Alumni Secretary

MARY BULLOCK
Advertising & Circulation

A MARINE AT GUADALCANAL

. . . pictured on the cover is Lieutenant Tom Dutton, '41. It's an official U. S. Marine Corps photo taken during the thick of things at Guadalcanal. Tom is now the Assistant Intelligence Officer at a secret South Pacific rest station, busy training other Intelligence officers and probably longing to see his newly born daughter, Jean Marcia. Mrs. Dutton is the former Elizabeth Tuckerman, '39.

In This Issue

Special Articles . . .

	PAGE
The Navy Invades Oberlin in July - - - - - - -	2
Oberlin in Uniform (Changes in Service Lists) - - - -	3
Freshman Sons and Daughters of Oberlin Alumni - - -	4
America and the Post War World	
5. Our Relations with South America, *by* J. Merle Davis, '99 -	5
Alumni Fund Off to Good Start - - - - - - -	8 and 20

Departments . . .

Under the Elms (Campus News) *by Jean Mills, '42* - - -	9
Athletics, *by W. I. Judson* - - - - - - - -	10
With the Faculty, *by Jean Mills, '42* - - - - - -	12
Alumni Club News - - - - - - - - -	14
"Ten Thousand Strong" (Class News) *Edited by Rebecca Bright* -	15

CREDIT FOR PHOTOGRAPHS

Cover—U. S. Marine Corps; pages 4, 11—A. E. Princehorn; page 12—Andrew Stofan; pages 18, 19, 20—U. S. Army; pages 17, 18—U. S. Navy.

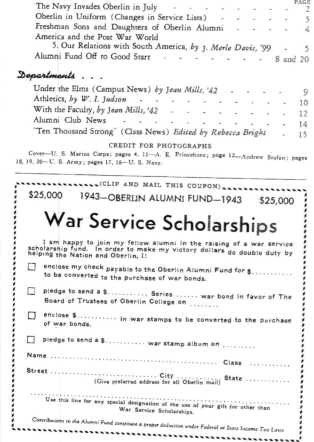
Only '93 and '98 Will Hold Formal Reunions

Oberlin College's bulletin announcing the complete program for Commencement, May 29-June 1, will be mailed to all alumni early in May.

It is expected that because of wartime difficulties only two classes will hold their regular reunions—the fifty year class, '93, at Elmwood Cottage, 117 Elm Street; and the class of '98 at Anchorage, 220 North Professor street.

However, Oberlin will welcome back all other alumni who may find it convenient to attend any of the Commencement events. May and June find the campus at its best— who could ever forget springtime in Oberlin?

Correcting Three Errors

In the March issue of the *Alumni Magazine*, under the pictures of the leaders of those classes which exceeded their 1942 Alumni Fund quotas, we inadvertently listed Mrs. Sara Atkinson Snyder, '41, of New York City simply as Mrs. Sara Atkinson.

Under the same group of pictures we made the error of listing Ernest Partridge, '95, when we should have listed D. Windzor Jones, '09, as the leader of a 100 per cent class.

Dr. Bill Tucker, '29, has called our attention to the fact that Emilie Ann Jones, '28, is a former business manager of the Oberlin *Review* and therefore the present manager, Mary Ellen Duffey, '44, is not the first woman to hold that position. We made the mistake of accepting the information from the *Review* without consulting our own memory which certainly would have told us better.

The Navy Invades Oberlin in July

SEVEN hundred thirty men, 30 of them Naval pre-meds and 700 in the Navy V-12 program, are expected in Oberlin on or about July 1. Final word that Oberlin College had been selected as a site for a Naval training school was received on April 5.

Many questions are being asked concerning the unit. Many of them cannot yet be answered. But perhaps a comprehensive statement of what has been done, what is being done, and of what is to be expected will help give a picture of the changes to be expected in Oberlin with the arrival of such a unit.

Of the 730 Navy men expected here for the summer term, 100 will be Oberlin men now enrolled in the Navy V-1 and V-7 programs. These reserves will stay on in Oberlin as members of the V-12 unit.

According to President Wilkins, present expectations are that the unit for the summer term will be made up as follows:

1) Oberlin men now in V-1 and
   V-7 ---------------------- 100
2) Men from other colleges now
   in V-1 and V-7 ----------- 484
3) and 4) Entering freshmen
   and men now in the Navy _ 146
                               ———
                               730

College authorities expect to receive early in June the records of the work done in other colleges by the students who are to be transferred here as members of V-12. Entering freshmen will have qualified for V-12 through the tests given throughout the country on April 2. They will begin a strictly prescribed curriculum, and all their work will be prescribed as long as they remain here.

The group of 700 men on the general program will consist in part of prospective aviation candidates and in part of prospective deck officers. Among those who enter the V-12 course as freshmen, the aviation cadets will spend two sixteen week terms here; the prospective deck officers will spend four sixteen week terms; and the pre-medical students will spend five sixteen-week terms here. Students already in college may, of course, finish their V-12 work in shorter periods.

The prescribed program for those who enter the V-12 course as freshmen consists in the first two terms of work in mathematics, English, history, physics, engineering drawing, Naval organization, and physical training.

The general V-12 program for the third and fourth terms comprise courses in navigation and nautical astronomy, chemistry, physics, mathematics, Naval history and strategy, psychology, and physical training. The course prescribed for pre-medical students is not unlike the course such students naturally follow in any college.

All members of the unit will have been selected for it as being potential officer material. They will not receive commissions on completion of their work here; but the intention of the Navy is that they shall have been so well qualified by their work here that after a certain amount of work in the Navy itself they will be ready for commissions.

At least seven new appointments of instructors are expected to be voted upon by the executive committee of the trustees on April 27. They will be appointments for four instructors in physics, to take effect July 1; one instructor in physics, effective November 1; 1 instructor in mathematics, effective July 1; 1 instructor in engineering drawing, effective July 1.

The colleges training these units will set examinations for the various courses given according to their own practices. Also, the usual scholastic standards of the institution will prevail. Near the end of the second term the Navy Department will give a qualifying examination of its own to all students.

The year's work will be divided into three sixteen-week terms, one beginning about July 1, one beginning about November 1, and one beginning about March 1. The college faculty voted to adopt this same schedule for the regular sessions. The coming summer session is scheduled to begin on July 1 and to end October 21; the winter session will begin on October 28 and will end on February 24 (with a nine-day vacation at Christmas time) and the spring session will begin on March 2 and end on June 22.

It will be permissible for students in the Navy unit and civilian students to attend the same classes. Students in the Navy unit will be permitted to participate in college athletics and other extra curricular activites insofar as it does not interfere with their prescribed courses or hours of study.

The men of the unit will be in uniform while here with pay and under Navy discipline and command. The Navy will send a commanding officer, who will probably arrive about the first

of June, and will probably send a medical officer, and probably one other commissioned officer, as well as three or four chief petty officers.

All men who are to serve as commandants for V-12 units are now taking a special course at Columbia University to prepare for this work. The assignment of commandants to colleges has not yet been made, but will probably be made about the middle of May.

On the 14th and 15th of May a conference will be held in New York City to be attended by the presidents of all V-12 colleges and the prospective commandants.

The men will be housed in Noah, the Men's Building, the Quadrangle, Talcott, and Baldwin. The Navy has asked that 230 men be put in the Men's Building, 150 in the Quadrangle, Noah, and Talcott, and 75 in Baldwin. No changes will need be made in these buildings as far as room needed to house the men, although several partitions between sections are being torn down. The men in excess of the number usually handled in those buildings will be cared for by the use of double deck beds. The Navy is furnishing 200 such beds. They will furnish, also, 375 desks, 375 chairs, and 755 lamps, as well as bedding for the men.

The men will eat, cafeteria system, at the Quadrangle, Baldwin, and Talcott. Plans have been made for necessary changes in the dining rooms of those three buildings to set up a cafeteria system. All of these plans are still subject to approval by the Navy. Generally the plan is as follows: the men will enter by one door, go through the line, receiving their food, and will eat at the regular long tables used in Navy "messes." They will then leave by another door, having left their trays at designated places. They will eat in two shifts at each dining room, making it possible for the Quadrangle to care for 300 men, Talcott 256, and Baldwin 200. These figures total over the 730 men Oberlin was allotted because the Navy has asked that they be prepared to feed and house up to about 755 men.

The Women's Old Gymnasium will be turned over for use as a storehouse for food and issue material for the unit. It is planned that the Commandant's office will be in this building, also. Workmen already are busy cleaning the gymnasium and installing new equipment.

Plans for the location of civilian students who under normal conditions would have been assigned to the buildings the unit will take over, are not yet complete. It is clear, however, that there will be room in college residences for as many women as are in college at present. Lord and Allencroft will be used as residences for freshmen women in place of Talcott.

Walter Webb Killed in Action; George Manlove and Norm Lyle Suffer Minor Wounds

The latest war casualties among Oberlin alumni, according to incomplete reports, include one death and two minor woundings.

It is reported that Walter G. Webb, x'40, of Teaneck, New Jersey, was killed in action in Tunisia. No further information has been received. Webb attended Oberlin from 1936 to 1938. He was a member of the YMCA cabinet in his sophomore year and was active in intramural sports. He was last listed in the alumni records in February 1941 as a store manager trainee in the McCrory Store at Allentown, Pennsylvania.

If the report is correct, Webb is probably the first Oberlin man to be killed in action in this war. Lieutenant Ralph I. Musson, x'39, of the Army Air Forces was reported missing in February in the Pacific combat area. Air Cadets Alexander D. Ross, '38, and Robert A. Baker, '39, were killed in December 1941 and April 1942 respectively, in training accidents. Colonel Charles M. Cummings, x'17, died just a week before our entrance into the war, at Lisbon, Portugal, while en route home from London on a secret military mission.

Lieutenant George Manlove, '36, was wounded in the hip by shrapnel while fighting in North Africa in March, and has been cited for the Order of the Purple Heart. However, Lieutenant Manlove wrote his parents that the wound was so slight that he did not even have time to get his clothes off to have it examined until seven more days of fighting had passed.

Lieutenant Norman Lyle, '42, a former editor of the Oberlin Review now flying with the U. S. Army Air Forces in the Alaskan combat area, was slightly wounded while in action on February 25. He is now recovered.

PICTURES WANTED

The editors urge all Oberlin alumni to forward immediately all available pictures of Oberlin graduates or former students who are now in the armed forces, for possible use in the Alumni Magazine. Informal group pictures are particularly welcome.

OBERLIN IN UNIFORM

One Month's Additions and Changes in Service Lists

NOTE: Included in the following list of Oberlin graduates and former students now in the armed forces are only those names (including changes of rank) which have been newly reported since the March issue of the Alumni Magazine. The complete list now numbers approximately 1250.

MEN

CLASS OF 1913
Metcalf, Franklin P. Maj AAF

CLASS OF 1918
Kindell, Nolan Capt USN

CLASS OF 1920
Meck, Floyd S. Lt Comdr USNR

CLASS OF 1925
Peirce, Wilmot W. MC USA

CLASS OF 1926
Holbein, Francis W. Corp AAF

CLASS OF 1927
Hansel, Robert J. Capt USA
Street, Francis E. Lt (jg) USNR

CLASS OF 1928
Schmidt, Hans W. Maj USA

CLASS OF 1929
Creighton, George M. Pfc USA
Wherley, Harold F. Capt MC USA

CLASS OF 1930
Barber, Hollis W. Lt USNR
Keeler, Harvey H. S/Sgt AAC

CLASS OF 1931
Hawkins, Roger R. USMM
Parker, Alfred A. USMM

CLASS OF 1932
Bohrer, Laurence E. Lt FA USA
Henry, Robert D. Pvt USA
Olmstead, John G. Corp USA

CLASS OF 1933
Bolbach, Robert L. Lt USNR
Schneider, August Z. Lt (jg) USNR

CLASS OF 1934
Heiser, Merle F. Ens USNR
Morrison, Daniel S. Cand USA
Wilbur, Halsey H. M. Y2c USNR

CLASS OF 1935
Chesler, David J. Lt MC USA

CLASS OF 1936
Cornman, W. Ivor Pfc MC USA
Goulder, N. Ernest Lt MC USA

CLASS OF 1937
Boycheff, Kooman A/C AAC
Friedman, Joseph R. Cand USA
Winner, Carl I. Cadet USCG

CLASS OF 1938
Avery, Charles W. Corp MC USA
Baughman, John W. x Pfc AAC
Harrison, Robert W. Ens USNR
Sokol, William Pvt USA
Sutherland, Sanborn Lt CE USA

CLASS OF 1939
Bennett, Bruce L. Lt (jg) USNR
Mills, Guy S. x. Pfc AAF
Potter, A. David Pvt Sig C USA

CLASS OF 1940
Bare, John K. T/Sgt USA
Barnhart, Frank E.
Byerley, Donald H. Ens USNR
Carroll, Rene Cand USA
Johnson, Walter C. Tech Inf USA
McConlogue, Raymond L. Ens USNR
Schmidt, F. Rudolph Capt AAC
Stevens, Howard M. Lt USA
Wilcox, Robert C. x, Corp Inf USA

CLASS OF 1941
Bradley, William L. Sgt AAC
Creighton, Joseph R. Lt QMC USA
DeMott, John J. Lt AAF
George, Wilbur S. CA(AA) USA
Greer, Robert T. Sgt USA
Hoagland, John H. Mid USNR
Parker, Frank C. Lt AAC
Schmidt, Carl M. Pvt AAC
Shell, Ralph E. Pfc Inf USA

WOMEN

Anderson, Elizabeth N. x'41, Ens WAVES
Brandt, Eleanor M. '32, WAVES
Carson, Edith M. '23, Lt (jg) WAVES
Cline, Charlotte M. '41, WAVES
Layman, Mrs. Emma McCloy, '30, Mid WAVES
Reedy, Mrs. Annesta Friedman, x'38, A/S WAVES
Rothrock, Bettina L. x'41, WAVES

CLASS OF 1942
Atherton, John P. A. Pvt Inf USA
Balcomb, John D. Corp CA(AA) USA
Bartow, John H. Ens USNR
Bohrer, Kenneth A. x, Sgt AAF
Brown, George C. Pfc Inf USA
Dice, Stanley F. A/C AAF
Lyon, Bayard W. Mid USNR
Saint, William S. S/Sgt USA
Worden, J. Stanley Ens USNR

CLASS OF 1943
Augustine, Thomas Lt AAC
Farnsworth, Charles E. Pvt FA USA
Hansen, James E. Pfc AAF
Higbie, Nathan B. Pfc AAF
Morris, VanCleve A/S USNR
Rees, Albert E.
Thorne, Robert S.
Wilson, John B. Pfc TSS USA

CLASS OF 1944
Cook, Peter F. Corp USA
Faragher, John H. Cand USA
Farley, Donald C. Pfc USA
Gordon, Lester E. Pvt AAF
Peterson, Harold W. Pvt AAF
Ross, Charles R. Sgt AAF
Skillings, Robert F.
Tischbein, Harry J. Pfc Inf USA

CLASS OF 1945
Abrahams, Morton S. Pvt USA
Backman, Carl W. Pvt Inf USA
Bassett, John P. Pvt Inf USA
Brunner, Robert O.
Chandler, Robert W. Pvt CA USA
Clifford, William Pvt AAF
Cochran, Harry C. Pvt AAF
Cook, George G.
Cummings, Abbott L.
Darbishire, Shelby W. A/S USNR
Dunham, Chester G.
Fabish, John G. Pvt AAC
Horvath, William L.
Maurice, Andre C.
O'Connor, William E. Pfc AAC
Silverburg, William J.
Smith, W. Duane
Wallace, William C.
Zimmerman, John L. Pvt AAC

CLASS OF 1946
Applebee, Roger K. A/S USNR
Bosworth, Edward I. A/S USNR
Dalgety, William D.
Dewey, Edward C.
Fink, Albert Pvt CA(AA) USA
Fowler, David H.
Frazer, Arthur L.
Knapp, William G.
Kuhne, Warner J.
Overly, A. Robert
Reinthal, Robert J.
Rosenthal, Vincent A.
Steinem, William A.
Stewart, Charles L.
Sunshine, James K.
Walton, Robert G.
Webber, George H. A/S USNR
Weiner, Bernard Pvt USA
Wright, Glenn R. Pvt AAC
Yeager, Leland B.

Freshmen Sons and Daughters of Oberlin Graduates

... these are the not-very-flattering identification pictures snapped of each new student within a day or two after his arrival on campus. Pictured are members of the June, October and February freshman classes who are children of Oberlin graduates. Though there are several freshmen with parents who are former students, these are not pictured. For a key to the pictures see the opposite page.

AMERICA AND THE POST WAR WORLD

5. Our Relations with South America

by J. Merle Davis, '99

T HE WAR has brought Latin America into the center of attention of North Americans. The notable series of inter-American political conferences of the past two decades, the invaluable work of the Pan American Union for hemispheric solidarity, and the scientific conferences and academic exchanges effected by research and peace foundations have for many years created a growing understanding of their neighbors among thoughtful circles in both Americas.

The world war has laid a violent hand upon the way of life of the common man of the whole Western hemisphere and has brought home to the masses of Americans, North and South, a sense of their common danger, their need of one another, and the inescapable solidarity of their interests. The crisis has also made millions of South and North Americans desire to know one another better. The spade work in inter-American cooperation that has gone before has laid the foundation for progress, but the present conflict creates an entirely new base line from

A profound student of international affairs, J. Merle Davis, '99, is Director of the Department of Social and Economic Research and Counsel of the International Missionary Council. His important personal studies in Africa, Asia and South America have been made the basis for the Council's plans for future work in those areas. He has recently returned from South America.

which the structure of future hemispheric solidarity may rise.

Praises Rockefeller's Office

In creating the Office of Coordinator of Cultural Relations with Latin America, the United States Government has taken a most important step in guiding the inevitable rapprochement of the Americas toward constructive and permanent ends. Though much of its economic and scientific program is affeered by the exigencies of the war and the immediate needs of the Allied nations, the basic strategy of the Coordinator's office is concerned with the shape of things to come in the Americas and the quality as well as form of the great structure of human society which will be erected upon the Western hemisphere. Scarcely any area of the life of the Latin American nations is being neglected by the Coordinators'

program: the undeveloped resources in ore, metals, petroleum, rubber, timber, and agriculture are being explored and tested; the water power and the possibilities of industrial development; the extension of transport facilities in railways, roads, waterways, and airways; financial loans and trade adjustments; questions of competitive and supplementary markets and the food requirements of the two continents; studies are under way on the fauna and flora, insect life, parasites, and pests endangering both plant and human life; the fields of new skills and cottage industries; sociological problems, such as housing, wages, diet, standards of living, migrations, the family system and social groupings; health and disease, sanitation, hygiene, undernourishment, and child welfare; the cultural inheritance —music, drama, ballads, folklore, proverbs, languages, dances, poetry, and literature; anthropological and ethnological investigations of the primitive Indians. This colossal program is based upon the determination of a great government to make the life of the two continents more intelligible to their people. On the other side of the balance sheet, the Coordinator's office has undertaken to interpret the way of life of the people of the United States to Latin America. Elaborate publications are issued; a comprehensive radio network has been set up; motion pictures are being prepared and displayed; entertainers, musicians, artists, and lecturers are being circuited; and translations of American literature into Spanish and Portuguese are being made.

In 1942 the course of five months of observation in the River Plate countries and Brazil, personal contact with a number of these economic, sociological, and health specialists impressed me with the high quality and thoroughness of their work. There can be no doubt that this great volume of trained observation will yield an unprecedented fund of knowledge and much understanding of the resources of our southern neighbors and the conditions under which they live.

The difficulty in this heroic effort is that, with nations as with persons, such

---

KEY TO FRESHMAN PICTURES ON OPPOSITE PAGE

Listed Below Are Each Student's Name and the Names of the Parents Who Are Oberlin Graduates

TOP ROW (left to right): Evelyn C. Adams of West Lawn, Pennsylvania—Florence Kriebel Adams, '15; Harrol W. Baker, Jr., of Lakewood, Ohio—Harrol W. ('17) and Virginia Johnson Baker, '20; Jane W. Bennett of Maumee, Ohio—Leonard P. ('16) and Margaret Dewey Bennett, '15; Edward I. Bosworth of Oberlin, now of the U. S. Navy—Edward F. Bosworth, '16; Donald L. Burneson of Oberlin, now of the U. S. Army—Lloyd W. ('19) and Ruth Parsons Burneson, '21; Donald P. Cameron of Racine, Wisconsin—Donald H. ('18) and Charlene Sebern Cameron, '18.

SECOND ROW: Alan S. Chaney of Rocky River, Ohio—Edwin H. ('19) and Mary Snively Chaney, '18; Mary K. Cheffy of Barnesville, Ohio—Helen Worthington Cheffy, '18; Barbara Ann Clarke of Shaker Heights, Ohio—Claude E. ('13) and Celia Scoby Clark, '13; Jean Cooley of East Palestine, Ohio—Mary Brown Cooley, '18; Margaret Cratt of Brattleboro, Vermont— Mary Luethi Cratt, '17; Miriam Daniels of Madison, Wisconsin—Olive Bell Daniels, '13.

THIRD ROW: Carol C. Davis of East Cleveland, Ohio—Hortense Mitchell Davis '16; William Dinkins of Selma, Alabama— Almedia Burwell Dinkins, '15; Gretchen Engstrom of Edgewood, Pennsylvania— Gertrude Schuchman Engstrom, '18; Catherine Fauver of Lorain, Ohio—the late Richard R. Fauver, '17; Evelyn Gott of Buffalo, New York—Frank R. ('09) and Cora Prefert Gott, '12; Jane Gray of West Hartford, Connecticut—Francis E. Gray, '17.

FOURTH ROW: Jean Hurd of Lisbon, Ohio—Elaine Van Fossen Hurd. '08; Philip T. Kelly of Scarsdale, New York—Marguerite Trunkey Kelly, '19; Sarah Catherine Langley of East Amherst, New York—Lucie Root Langley, '17; Anne Latourette of Milford, Michigan—Sheldon H. ('12) and Margaret Bennett Latourette, '12; Sarah Lorenz of Toledo, Ohio—Alice Barber Lorenz, '12; William L. Lyon of Chicago, Illinois—Dr. Will Ferson Lyon, '11.

FIFTH ROW: Jean T. MacArthur of Toronto, Ontario—John W. MacArthur, '10; D. Graham McCanns of Richmond, Indiana—Shirley Graham McCanns, '34; Charlotte Peters of Houston, Texas—the late Bertha Hickin Peters, '11; Robert A. Roth of Youngstown, Ohio—Marion Benjamin Roth, '19; Mary E. Sherman of Cincinnati, Ohio—Lucy McGormley Sherman, '11; W. Arthur Swan of Minden, Nebraska —Rev. Wilbur F. ('10) and Enid Sutton Swan, '15; Constance B. Weil of University Heights, Ohio—Carol Wallace Weil, '20; Nancy Williams of Grosse Point, Mich. igan—Paul D. ('16) and Eleanor Bell Wil. liams, '16; Robert W. Woodruff of La. Grange, Ohio—George W. ('15) and Fran. ces Starr Woodruff, '16; Janet S. Woodrow of Redlands, California—Hazel Silcox Woodrow, '21; Conrad V. Urban of Erie, Pennsylvania—Bernice Hoppa Urban, '22; Martha Jean Vogt of Akron, Ohio—Walter W. ('17) and Nellie Rennecker Vogt, '18.

BOTTOM: Patricia A. Yocom of Ober. lin—Herbert ('09) and Mary Willis Yo. cum, '15.

matters as living together and liking one another cannot be carried out under high pressure and are conditioned by factors which elude measurement.

Efforts Largely Unilateral

There are serious limitations to this intensive program for promoting the Good Neighbor policy: first, it is to a very large extent a unilateral program. The Coordinator's Office of Cultural Relations, like the Good Neighbor policy, is a child of the American administration. With characteristic Yankee drive, the child must be nursed to full stature in the shortest possible time. To this end unlimited funds and a small army of experts were speedily made available. Within a very short time offices were set up in nearly every Latin American capital, and the process of gathering data and interpreting culture was under way. However, the process is not reciprocal, and, although Latin Americans are attached to the Coordinator's offices in their various countries as advisers, their function is that of implementing a program already set up in Washington. Among the more than four hundred employees in the Coordinator's Washington office are only twenty Latin Americans, most of whom are translators, and only one representative of the twenty Latin American republics is employed as an adviser. Such procedure ignores the first principles of neighborliness and common sense.

Differences in Temperament

Again, the Coordinator's program violates some of the basic instincts of our southern neighbors. It is difficult for the North American to grasp the implications of the fact that people in the tropics have been born under a different mood of nature from men of the temperate zone. It is a mood which has created different values and different nervous reactions from those of the northerner. In tropical America the necessity to hurry is looked upon as a disaster, and hard work is considered a calamity to be avoided at all costs. There, time is not money but rather a medium of enjoyment, and life's satisfactions and status are not measured in bank balances but rather in terms of wide-sweeping haciendas and in numbers of well-fed cattle and under-fed peons. The Latin American tends to be amused and repelled by the deadly seriousness and drive with which his northern neighbor goes about the business of life, and particularly the business of cultivating friendship. The southerner looks upon friendship as the outgrowth of mutual interests and unhurried association of people who have time to sit together and drink many cups of *máte* and strong coffee and argue interminably over what to us seems matters of small consequence.

Differences in Wealth

A further difficulty in practicing the Good Neighbor policy inheres in the tremendous disparities in wealth, power, and material progress between the United States and nearly all of her southern neighbors. It is as difficult for a small and poor Latin American state to be on intimate terms of comradeship with a fabulously rich and powerful nation like the United States as it would be for a bricklayer and a millionaire to fraternize. The United States not only conceives a colossal plan but has unlimited funds and trained men for carrying it through. Her neighbors are, for the most part, nations of undeveloped resources which need vast amounts of capital for development. The rich neighbor has not only ample capital but has the organizational experience and scientific skill to exploit the poor neighbor's inheritance. Even should our southern neighbors have the finances and equipment to undertake an intensive investigation of North American resources and potentialities, it would be wasted effort; for these have long since been tabulated and absorbed into the American economic organization. Here again the Good Neighbor policy of proposed cooperation is unilateral, and like a one-way street whose only exit leads to direct concessions to the United States or to huge loans of capital and of expert management which would enhance the power of the big neighbor. A classic example is the case of Cuba, where one-half of the arable lands and two-fifths of the sugar estates are held by foreign capitalists, and seven-eighths of the public utilities and all the big banks are in North American hands.

Brazil, and every Latin American country except Argentina and Uruguay, faces a major dilemma at this point. Brazilians are awake to the immense potentialities of their huge domain; their natural resources, if developed, could support from ten to twenty times the present population. The ore, the land, the water power, and the climate all are available to create one of the mightiest nations on earth. However, the necessary capital can be secured only by foreign loans, for the Brazilian people are too poor to be taxed to this extent or to subscribe to the bond issues that would be required. Much of the experienced leadership for such development also would have to come from North America. Under these circumstances it is no wonder that Brazil responds to the friendly overtures of the United States, but that, at the same time, she is concerned over the possible implications of accepting the help of her powerful northern neighbor.

A Final Difficulty

A final difficulty in the way of a solidarity of understanding between North and South America lies in the orientation of their cultures. The culture of the Latin American nations has been rooted deep in European soil. Through the winning of their independence from Spain and Portugal, the political ties of these nations with Europe have long been severed, but the cultural ties still hold. At one extreme stands Argentina, still considering herself a European rather than an American nation and unwilling to cut her moorings to the European world even though it is falling in ruins. In contrast, Brazil, having cut both the political and cultural bonds that held her to Portugal, proudly considers herself 100 per cent an American nation.

A majority of our southern neighbors have been passing through a difficult adjustment in watching the world that nurtured them and gave them their culture, fall like a house of cards. The experience is yet more difficult since they know that in any Western hemispheric union of nations the United States will inevitably be the dominant power. The sources of mistrust of their northern neighbor are too recent, and in Argentina especially, the low estimate of American culture, manners, and way of life is too deep-seated happily to allow the United States to take the cultural place of Europe. Latin America is facing a spiritual and cultural crisis; the old landmarks have been destroyed, and it is too early to expect that she will immediately find her new bearings.

There is much of mutual misunderstanding and prejudice to overcome, which will require time and an intelligent sustained approach by all concerned: the different media of speech; the contrasted attitudes toward the rôle of women in society and in the home; the northern strictures upon the Latin double moral standard, matched by the southerner's scorn of American loose public morals as portrayed by Hollywood; and the implications for every human relationship inherent in the contrasted philosophy of the Napoleonic an English code of law.

Friendly Spirit Essential

In the face of these areas of friction it is becoming apparent that the nations of this hemisphere are consciously drawing together in a new solidarity and brotherhood, and that the forces which are drawing them together are stronger than those which keep them apart. If such controversial factors as competitive production, markets, tariffs, trade regulations, loans, and transportation facilities can be dealt with in a spirit of friendliness, as among good neighbors rather than as competitors, and if the principle of "each for all and all for each" can be realized, it may be possible for the conflicting economic interests and cultural frictions which have separated the Americas to fade into the background and a new era of mutual appreciation and solidarity to be entered.

The American nations have a common and sacred experience—the struggle against tyranny and the winning of their liberties; they have accepted the common task of subduing a new world and building in it a new human society. Now that tyranny again threatens their liberties and the structure they have erected, they are united in the defense of their common heritage and must face the solemn responsibility of building together a new and more worthy world.

Can Learn Much From South

In the fulfillment of that responsibility the twenty-one republics of the hemisphere need one another. If it is true that the Latin American lands need the economic and scientific resources and the creative energy of the United States, it is equally true that the great republic of the north needs to sit at the feet of her southern neighbors and learn from them. In matters of race the Latin American peoples have made a reality of the principle of liberty and equal opportunity, upon which we pride ourselves and which in practice we deny to one-tenth of our citizens; from the solidarity of the Latin family system the disintegrating North American family has much to learn, and, in the graciousness and leisure to cultivate good manners and the capacity to enjoy life rather than be driven by it, the northerner has one of the choicest arts of living to acquire. These things—racial tolerance, equality of opportunity, the solidarity of the family, and the exercise of the art of gracious living—are essentials of any civilization and are criteria of the worth and true greatness of a state.

The most stubborn obstacles in the path of our future relations with Latin America, and particularly in appreciating our neighbors, are not in either the political or economic spheres. They lie rather in ourselves and in the adjustment of our prejudices, ways of life, and ideology to that of our neighbors. Mother Nature, history, and environment have created two diverse streams of life and two contrasting patterns of society. There will be a basis for no more than a mutually superficial understanding and scant respect in the postwar community of the Americas until we modify our attitude toward color; until we find other criteria of respect

for peoples than economic and scientific efficiency, the size of their pay checks, their use of flush toilets, and the literacy and health of their masses. On the other hand, the Latin Americans must find other tests of our morality and culture than the bedroom scenes and gun play of our movies, the lynchings and Jim Crow discriminatory treatment of our Negro population, and the conditions prevailing among our sharecroppers and army of unemployed.

No nation in the world surpasses Brazil in the multi-racial strains of its people. Sixty races are present in its modern population. Portuguese is the basic stock, and with it are usually present varying admixtures of Negro or Indian blood. We met well-placed Brazilian families in whose veins flow the blood of eight distinct races. The people point to this unusual inheritance with a fine pride and grace, and it is clear that this is a source of the rare charm of the Brazilian.

Must Study Languages

The post-war period must provide that Spanish and Portuguese are required languages in our North American schools and colleges, and, in this way, match the provision for English teaching in the schools of several Latin American lands. English is studied by every Argentinian and Chilean pupil above the primary grade. Such language courses should be supplemented by provision for Spanish- and Portuguese-speaking circles in which our youth may be familiarized with the correct use of the spoken languages.

There must be a recognition of literature as the most effective road to an understanding of the soul and ideology of other people, and provision be made for the translation on a scale never before attempted of the best authors, essayists, poets, and philosophic and religious writers of the two continents.

The program of the International Institute for Cultural Relations, by which students and teachers are sent on an exchange plan to study in North and South America should be widely extended. In such exchanges, the main purpose of cultural understanding and of gaining an insight into the basic national values rather than technical training should be made central.

South American young people should be placed in our smaller colleges and universities where they may come close to the heart of American life, rather than be allowed to gain their impressions alone from the great state and metropolitan educational centers.

Increasingly, opportunities should be arranged for conferences of the youth of North and South America in which

the future leaders may exchange their thoughts upon a wide scope of mutual problems and become familiar with the quality of mind and points of view of their youthful neighbors.

Travel Exchanges

In arranging for travel exchanges, more attention should be given to the routing of parties to the smaller cultural centers and to rural areas, so as to give opportunity for observing all sides of the life of the countries visited including the quiet, generating sources of national strength and ideology, rather than concentrating upon the usual tourist round of travel in the great centers of population with their spectacular concentrations of power, luxury, and amusement.

Lectures by Latin American educators, scholars, artists, and public men and women should become a frequent part of lyceum programs in our towns, cities, and colleges; and, similarly, North Americans should be increasingly heard, if invited, in Latin American communities.

Suggests International Forum

Finally, the formation of an Institute of Inter-American Relations is suggested. This would be an unofficial forum of the peoples of the Americas. Such an institute would provide for the periodic meeting of representatives from many walks of life, including labor, agriculture, economics, business, education, science, medicine, women's organizations, and social welfare. An opportunity for unhurried discussion of matters of common interest, mutual concern, and international and interracial friction would be provided. The discussions would be informal in character and would represent no governmental or party interest. Supplementing such conference discussions and an outgrowth from them would emerge a continuous program of studies. These would be carried out cooperatively under the best scholastic leadership of the countries concerned, and would be related to the topics of liveliest interest and significance which developed in the periodic conferences of the Institute. The findings of such studies would be used as source material upon which discussions at subsequent conferences would be based. In this way, research would point up and strengthen discussion while discussion would indicate those fields upon which further research would be required. Such a procedure would gradually build up mutual understanding and friendship in many groupings of the people, and, by correcting misunderstandings, would tend to reduce tension areas and friction and would form a basis for a growing inter-American solidarity.

Alumni Fund Off to Good Start

OBERLIN'S 1943 Alumni Fund is off to a flying start with a total of $4,436.50 subscribed by 578 donors as of April 10. This figure represents all alumni giving through the Alumni Association. The larger part, $2,483.50, of this sum has been designated for special purposes such as the Jaszi Lectureship Fund, the Shansi Fund, the Class of '98 Fund, the Lord Scholarship Fund, etc.

The balance, $1,953.00, has been contributed to the General Alumni Fund, for which the goal this year is the raising of $25,000 for war-service scholarships. With this "nest egg" to work on, the Fund officers are looking forward to a successful year. Scholarships for men who left college for war service will be urgently needed at the close of the war and all alumni are urged to support this year's Fund.

Listed below are the names of donors to the various funds collected through the Alumni Association. It is hoped that those who have given for special purposes will also contribute to the war-service scholarships. This list is correct as of April 10. The names of new donors will appear in later issues.

PRIOR TO 1891
Henry L. Bates, '76; Charles J. Chamberlain, '88; Georgiana Mead Clarke, '87; Emilie Royce Comings, '77; Janette E. Corbin, '90; Jessie Cowles Fifield, x'89; Mary L. Fowler, '87; James H. Garnett, '83; William R. Green, '79; Mary Ingraham Heyward, '88; Lelia Johnson, '81; Mary Matter, '84; Mary Ellis Nichols, '85; Grace Mellen Rood, '90; Janet McKelvey Swift, '83; Lillie Thompson Terborgh, '88·

1891
Willard L. Beard, Mary Safford Campbell, Alice Jones Emery, Mary Harward Evans, Annis Mead Hunt, R. T. Miller, Jr.

1892
Inez Michener Smith, Cora Swift, Minerva Mitchell Wickliffe, Stephen R. Williams.

1893
Esther A. Close, Charles H. Nims.

1894
Kate Watson Forbes, Charles L. Stocker, Isaac Terborgh.

1895
James H. Davidson.

1896
John D. Harding, Jessie L. Shank.

1897
Harlan Dudley, John Heasele, Emma L. Lentz, Louis E. Lord, Ellen R. Raymond.

1898
Alberta Cory Crisman, Elsie B. Denham, James H. Griswold, John R. Kuns, Elizabeth Tarbox Lumbard, 'x, Albert C. Norris, Luera W. Schellbach, Harriet N. Schrader, Lucien T. Warner.

18899
Esther Ward Brown, Nellie Moorhead Dougal, Albert H. Eichach, Mary Williams Hemingway.

1900
Celestia Hanby Grant, Arthur J. Harvey, Martha Miller Harvey, Rose Munger Oviatt, Florence Voorhees Phinney, Mary E. Sinclair, Martha Storrs Swift.

1901
Berta H. Bowers, Edwin Brouse, Mabel Millikan Brown.

1903
Harvey Heebner, Elizabeth Willard Hope, Edith Hatch Ryan, Walter Ryan, Frank W. Vincent.

1904
John H. Angle, Ernest W. Atwater, George Reuben Brown, Olive Sieben Greenwood, Cassie Kelner Jackson, Carrie Lohnes Priebe.

1905
Merton E. Chamberlain, Grace M. Cox, Helen Abbott Douglas, Frances Knox Vincent.

1906
Goldie M. Bowser William S. Cochran, A. Beatrice Doerschuk, Trafton Dye, Bertha E. Hart, Edwin E. Millet John G. Olmstead, Franklin P. Schaffer, Lois D. Walker.

1907
Bernice Harper Brisebois, Mabel Bronson, Hiram S. Caldwell, Daisie Gehman Fairfield, Wynn Fairfield, Edwards D. Ford, Mary Parsons McCullough.

1908
Mary Hobbs, Mary Purcell Lester, Irma Lewis, George P. Metcalf, Mabel G. Whiting.

1909
Hazel Petty Payden, Edith Stimson Paterson, Elma Schultz, Ernest Van Fossan.

1910
William S. Ament, Carrie Benham, Jacob Bloomgarden, W. Spencer Bowen, Rachel Coss Cochran, Dorothy Fairchild Graham, Norma Hazeltine, Grace Leadingham, Louise Martin, Anna Osborn, Flora S. Scott, Howard T. Smith, Sadie G. Smith, Keim K. Tibbetts.

1911
Ethel Brubaker, Esther Robson Bowen, Miriam A. Conant, Lillian Dowler Eichbauer, Ara Scothan Loomis, W. Arthur McKinney, Adena Miller Rich, Harold Tower, Alfred G. Walton.

1912
Helen Dart, Clara L. Hathaway, Lucille Kalb Irwin, William Jackson, Willard S. Lines, Frances Cochran MacDaniels, Laurence MacDaniels, Harold P. Miller, Margaret Parsons, Dorothy R. Swift.

1913
Myrtle Kellogg Cheney, Walter L. Cheney, Lloyd H. Matteson, Paul T. Weeks, Eleanor Lassey Smith.

1914
Lester M. Beattie, Ruth Brown, Frank C. Fisher, Newton B. Green, Luther Gulick, Helen Swift Gulick, Lola Randall Pierce, Christine Bigelow Wright, Kathryn Stewart Yarborough.

1915
Florence Nichols Adams, Frieda Kriebel Adams, Eleanor Hill Ament, Charlotte Weatherill Bosworth, William P. Davis, Vesper Wood Davis, Mary Darst Driehorst, Henry H. Lichtwardt, Dora Clemmer Mathews, James V. Polacek, Mary Ingell Walton.

1916
E. Cowles Andrus, William D. Andrus, James Dunn, Sarah Bailey Dunn, Madeline P. Goodwin. Lawrence McAllister, Esther Schultz, Marie Rogers Vail, Florence M. Warner.

1917
Margaret H. Aylard, Edith M. Gates, Rudolf Hurtz, Florence A. Hiatt, Mary Vanderhoof Mulhanser, Harlan R. Parker, Mary F. Tenney, James A. Thomas, Myra I. Wade, Helen R. Watson, Pauline Zinninger.

1918
Alvina S. Burk, F. Frank Croll, Leo L. Du. ersun, Donald Forward, E. Althea Heimbach, Nira R. Kimmel, Florence Clisby Larson, Susie McCreery, Margaret Wright North, Jessie Raine Portmann.

1919
Harold W. Baker, Katharine Bard Battelle, Rose M. Dolezal, Harmon H. Flinkers, Helen Anderson Hamilton, Herbert Lansdale, Jr., Marian W. Mair, Helen Murray, Alice Leuthi Wil. lianis.

1920
Helen L. Carter, Edna Dana, Josephine Dunn, Lorine K. Grosz, Lottie Bose Porter, Riba Gobel Shai, Marian Treat.

1921
Margaret Barnard, Geraldine Beard, Wilson J. Clark, Melvin A. Dietrich, Carroll P. Lahman, Hazel Robinson Lahman, Charles Lauthers, Helen Williams LePontois, Mary Sitler Miller, Raymond T. Moyer, Glen W. Nethercut, Josephine E. Roberts, Grace Arnold Spillane, Helen Eimert Stoertz, Harold N. Williams.

1922
Dorothy Burton, Margaret G. Chapin, Gertrude Layman Churchill, H. Louise Converse, Frances Kilts Holaday, Birdie H. Holloway, Ruth Kelley Montgomery, Bertha Phelps, G. Miriam Spreng, Dorotha L. Whitney.

1923
A. Jeanette Beebe, Helen Harris Denny, Jenny Parr Georgette, Sidney Gulick, Jr., Francis S. Hutchins, Garnet J. Knights, Stanley Meck, Lois R. Robinson.

1924
Anna Wood Armstrong, Evelyn Buck, Kathryn M. Carey, Theodore Erikson, Mary E. Gilcrist. Ruth Hubbard, Dortha Salisbury Leonard, Gretta Bellows Schirmer.

1925
Dorothy Raymond Crawford, Lucille H. Fitch, Erwin N. Griswold, Charlotte Ludlum, Velma Seale Mentzer, Earl R. Moses, Ethel Yokes Ogden, Ethel Scott Phipps, Glenn R. Rodgers, Helen Eaton Roudebush, Ruth K. Wyse.

1926
Mary Louise Ainsworth, Evelyn Sheldon Baxter, Louise Harrington Busey, Eva Taylor Cowan, Clermont P. Doane, Robert W. Dobbin, Esther Haynes Dobbins, Elias J. Elctier, Lucy

Ruth Bullock Boynton Is Fund's Vice Chairman

Ruth Bullock (Mrs. Arthur J.) Boynton, '08' of Winnetka, Illinois, has accepted the position of Vice Chairman of the 1943 Alumni Fund. She joins Chairman Whiting Williams, '99' in leading this year's Fund for war service scholarships.

Mrs. Boynton has been active both in alumni and community affairs since her graduation. While an undergraduate she was Vice President of the class in her junior year, a member of the Hi-O-Hi Board, and President of Baldwin Cottage. For many years she was Class Councillor for 1908 and is now Vice President of the Chicago North Shore Women's Club.

Among the numerous officerships of local and community groups which Mrs. Boynton has held are the presidency of the 21 Neighborhood Circles of Winnetka, presidency of the Woman's Society of the Winnetka Community Church, vice presidency of the Winnetka Parent-Teachers Association and chairmanship of the Department of International Cooperation of the League of Women Voters.

Two of Mrs. Boynton's daughters, Margaret, x'31, and Sylvia, x'36, attended Oberlin. Margaret is a Wellesley graduate. Her sister, Mrs. Charles P. (Sylvia Boynton) Ainsworth, graduated in 1923.

M. Hertzog. Francis W. Holbein, Janet McLennan Kerr, Herbert N. Noble, Harris E. Phipps, Robert Powell, Verna Christophel Riggs, Eva Lee Sackett, Charlotte Payne Segur, Norman R. Shaw, Maren Thomsen Stewart, Elizabeth Walker, Helen Templeton Young.

1927

Paul Bezazian, Jacob Clayman, Robert R. Crawford, William C. Eichelberger, H. Eugenia Hart, Paul E. Lees, Wilbert Montie, John Pivaroff, 'x. James Roemer, Hestor Simpson, Andrew C. Westervelt.

1928

William M. Bennett, Jr., Luella Eisenmann Brown, Elizabeth Craig, Irene Ziegler Hill, Alfhild J. Johnson, Emilie Jones, Harold Jones, Charles A. Mosher, S. Norman Park, George L. Partridge, Louis S. Peirce, Jerry McCord Roberts, Carroll K. Shaw, Conna Bell Shaw, Elizabeth Zorbaugh Smith.

1929

Charles J. Adler, Kathryn Childs Cassidy, Gertrude Jacob, Eunice Kettering, A. Jeannette Moore, Maggie Winstead Powell, Helen MacAllister Reeder, Clarence Y. Shimamura,

1930

Carl Allensworth, Donald L. Baker, O. Leonard Brandes, Robert W. Cairns, Harold G. Cassidy, Ruth Kleinbohl Clarke, Bernard L. Gladieux, Jonas H. Hemsing, Virginia Thatcher Hoecker, Elinor Moore Irvin, Marian L. Lord, Kenneth G. McDaniel, Walter P. Rogers, Harriet Crosby Sheridan, Hilton A. Smith, Magrieta Livingston Wilson.

1931

Jean Ball, Beryl Spicer Brandes, Jane Smith Brush, Katherine Kuhn Cairns, Roger A. Clapp, Ernest M. Dickerman, Muriel Hanson Elliott, Rolland J. Gladieux, Elizabeth S. Hanson, Vivienne Haring, Susan Shedd Hemingway, Edward S. Peck, Louise Hutchinson Olmstead, Edwin O. Reischauer, Ruth Sheppard Searle, Caroline Schulz Service, John S. Service, Ranghild Nelson Stone, Ruth Cross Utley, R. Benjamin Whiting.

1932

Margaret Auten Beveridge, Harriet Reid Clapp, Martha Woodmancy Deraw, Oliver Crummitt, Laurene Turnbull Heiman, Amy Kramers Hill, Kathleen Reed Joseph, Mousheng Lin, Frank C. Locke, Kathrine C. McCullough, Laura Mick Moore, Stanbery Nichols, M. Isabel Smith, Hubert P. Stone.

1933

Frederick F. Bauer, Mary McKee Davies, Jane Morrison Dickerson, Helen H. Grant, Faith Fitch Hill, Ernest Hutcheson, Dorothy Rainer Kamm, Harriet McCullough Kistler, Marian Conant McPherson, Sarah H. Metcalf, Henry A. Mosher, Nancy Millette Mosher, Herman Petricoff, Ruth Mick Schloemer, Jeanne Hibbard Stephens, Eleanor Buell Walter.

1934

R. Williams Bell, George W. Biro, Helen Clapesattle, Robert Y. Durand, Doris L. Flierl, Beatrice M. Green, Frances Cade Hamlin, Anna Koglin, Daniel S. Morrison, Ruth A. Moulton, Ruth Coates Roush, Mary Brown Spicer, Elizabeth Snow.

1935

Donald C. Allen, Josephine Peirce Brown, David J. Chesler, Charles O. Duff 'x, Helen A. Fanning, Dorothy Pierce Hamilton, John N. Hamilton, Michael Hoffman, William Howell, Jr., Marjorie Hubbard, Robert W. Hunt, Frances Lowell Kipp, Eleanor Loomis Noback, Isabel Clark Sanders, Esther F. Schmidt, Phillip B. Shuman, Arthur S. Tucker.

1936

Jane Adriance Ailey, Robert J. Ailey, Richard A. Aszling, Henry M. Boardman, Marjorie Skinner Boardman, Bonnie A. Dunlop, Abram B. Goldstein, Charles W. Gould, Jeanne B. Graber, Leroy P. Graf, John Hamlin, Katherine Hughes Hoffman, William C. Kidd, Philip Mayer, Uel P. McCullough, Harriet Wright Miller, Lucien E. Morris, Myron H. Nichols, Lamoyne Pay, David H. Pinkney, Joseph S. Ransmeier, Lucille Dorn Shaw, Jane S. Wagner, Don H. Williams, Mary deSchweinitz Wood.

1937

Margery V. Aber, Aileen Strong Allen, Martha Barry, Lillis Baker Carson, Lydia Symons Dubin, Frieda Wilson Ellsworth, Pauline L. Guscott, Roger G. Hamilton, Edwin Kinder. man, Joanna Knowlton Lucas, Mary Cleaver May, Barbara Mearns, Frances E. Morgan,

UNDER THE ELMS

by Jean Mills, '42

Nisei Boy Elected President Of New Student Council

Kenji Okuda, junior from Seattle, Washington, has been elected president of the student council, succeeding Elmer Engstrom.

Okuda, an American-born U. S. citizen of Japanese descent, came to Oberlin in February from the Granada Relocation Project, Lamar, Colorado, after he had been released for college study by the War Relocation Authority. He had attended the University of Washington for five quarters, where he was an honor student and vice-president of the Y. M. C. A.

Soon after his arrival in Oberlin he took part in a chapel discussion on the problem of Japanese relocation. His able presentation of the problem as he saw it, after having spent several months in a relocation camp, made an excellent impression upon the student body and was largely responsible for his being nominated to run for the position of president of the student council.

The platform on which he was elected urged the extension of the activities of the Student War Council and full utilization of college men and women to meet the farm labor shortage.

Okuda, who is majoring in economics, is interested in teaching as a future occupation. He is, also, greatly interested in and anxious to be a part of plans for rebuilding the world after this

war. While at the Granada Relocation Project he was active in the college-age group of men and women, helping to sponsor activities and to build up a college catalogue library, and securing college papers for use there.

Faculty and Student Groups Help Farmers Husk Corn

Land Army activities of students this spring have brought praise from farmers around Oberlin. The students, men and women, have been helping to husk corn at nearby farms, corn that stood all winter because abnormally wet weather last fall prevented husking.

Their assistance has been of great value to the farmers, who are unable to hire extra help due to the manpower shortage. Without part-time help planting would be seriously delayed.

Faculty members, also, have returned to the land, and early in April five of them husked corn all day at the farm of Eugene Babcock, '17' and his wife, Esther Shelton Babcock, '21' The crew that day included Professors Reuel Frost, George T. Jones, Erwin Stumm, Dan Kinsey and J. R. Reichard. Among members of the Oberlin Rotary Club who have husked several times (once in a blizzard) were Dudley Barnard, '30' Charles Meek, '38' Professor Victor Lytle, '12' C. A. Mosher, '28' and Professors Alfred Schlesinger and Roger Shaw.

(Under Elms continued, Page 11)

Phyllis A. Pearson, Dorothy Platt, Marjorie Batson Plume, Margaret Wilson Redick, Robert Schloemer, James C. Scofield, Elizabeth W. Smith, Margaret Stanion, Charlotte Tinker, Frances E. Unkefer, Wilfred H. Ward, Phyllis Agate Wentz, June Stockfish Wing, Dorothy Witr.

1938

Perry R. Ayres Mabel W. Brown, Sanford Dubin, Marian R. Emerine, Jean Filkins, Gilbert R. Fischer, Barbara Willits Fitts, Helen M. Foster, James C. Goodrich; Kathleen Thompson Harbaugh, Will M. Heiser, James H. Hubbell, Elizabeth Ann Hull, Melville Kennedy, Richard R. Lyman, Anne Love McKown, Charles J. Meek, Christine Miller, Margaret Phillips, Janet Brown Schwertman, Ruth E. Ward, Ruth E. West.

1939

Bruce L. Bennett, Donald Berkemeyer, Elizabeth Tuckerman Dutton, James D. Guernsey, Merle R. Hoddinott, Doris Kempes, Jerome Klein, Nancy Merrill, Albert S. Millman, Elizabeth G. Mills, Frances Harvey Moran, Janet E. Nash, Frances Pauls, Harriet Dexter Pennington, Arnold J. Sagalyn, Ross Sanderson, Carl J. Schneider, John B. Schwertman, Robert W. Sharp, Robert S. Vogel.

1940

Harold E. Brailey, Ruth Rawlinson Bergengren, Giles G. Blodgett, M. Elizabeth Bridenbaugh, William L. Cash, Robert M. Comfort, Donald W. Flierl, Georgene E. Griffith, Mary Taylor Hinkey, Robert T. Kretchmar, William M. Moore, Elton Mosher, Virginia R. Norris, Jean Gleason Pell, Charlotte Philleo, Evelyn

Edwards Rorick, Velma Mears Walton, Barbara Wells.

1941

Harriet D. Adair, J. Gordon Bennett, William L. Bradley, Nancy J. Brewster, Leo Bronsky, Alexander Brooks, Frederick M. Douglas, Jr., Robert C. Duncan, Thomas C. Dutton, Irving Foote, Robert D. Fleischer, Elizabeth Koski Heikkinen, John F. Hersh, M. Katherine Hunt, John B. Kidd, Barbara King, Virginia Lane. Virginia Cole Little, Helen U. Martin, Donald J. McGrew, Frank Picket, Lois C. Shelton, Edward O. Tabor, Jr., Alexander Ware, Delores Wennerstrom.

1942

Eleanor J. Antes, Virginia N. Baker, Grace W. Chap, Joy Coombs, Jessie Starr Crane, Charles L. Dunn, A. Hunter Dupree, Herbert E. Hansen, Margaret Helseth Hobbs, John A. Hunt, Irving C. Jackson, Ellen W. MacDaniels, William T. Martin, Jr., Daniel Meloy, Nancy G. Miller, Dorothy Morris, Vincent Price, Andrey Meacham Schwinn, Margaret Smith, James M. Stengle, Victor J. Stone, A. Prentice Van Derstine, J. Carol Zimmerman.

FRIENDS AND FORMER STUDENTS

Ethel Parsons Anuis, x'07; Ruth B. Calvin, '43; Brooks Emeny, John F. Fairfield, x'44; William Fishback, '43; Gloria C. Gordon, '44; William E. Hawkes, x'43; Cecelia M. Kenyon, '43; David R. Moore, Emily B. Purvis, '44; Albert E. Rees, '43; Jewell C. Stradford, '43; Edward O. Tabor, Philip Tear, '43.

CLUBS

Chicago Women's Club.

ATHLETICS

by W. J. Judson

Split Even in Opening Double Header at Ohio Wesleyan

The Yeomen opened their 1943 season at Ohio Wesleyan, April 17, dropping the first game of a twin bill, 5-2, and winning the nightcap, 2-1.

Sophomore Bob Houser, pitching his first intercollegiate game in the opener, got off to a shaky first inning when two walks, an error and three straight hits gave the Bishops their five runs.

Friedl Anders, veteran moundsman, pitched one of the best games of his collegiate career in the nightcap, striking out 12 and limiting the opposition to two singles, one in the first inning and the other in the sixth. Wesleyan scored their lone run in the opening inning when an error put their lead-off man on base and later scored on the first of their two hits.

Spicer's Single Scores Two

The Yeomen waited until the final inning to put on the winning rally, being hitless and behind 1-0 until that time. Bob Zunzer, Dick Clewell and Bill Diehl all laid down perfect bunts to fill the bases in the eventful seventh. At that point Captain Russ Spicer lined a hart-hit single down the left field foul line to score both Zunzer and Clewell and ice the game.

An attack of tracheitis kept Coach Throner at home and Dr. Herb Nichols who was in charge of the trip stated, "They were two of the best collegiate games I have ever seen. Both teams had very few errors and the Yeomen played an excellent defensive brand of ball."

Prospects Are Good

Although only four of last year's lettermen are back, Oberlin's prospects seem fairly bright for a successful baseball season. Sophomore Bill Tuck, captain-elect of next year's basketball team, probably will be at first, Captain Russ Spicer at short, Bob Zunzer on second and Eugene Wehrli on third. Bill Fletcher has been working at the backstop position, although Bill Tuck could also alternate at that spot.

In the outfield, lettermen Hugh Kernohan and Dick Clewell will probably roam in left and center field, while either Paul Scranton or John Arbour may be in right field. Other good outfield prospects include John Anderson, Bob Keesey, and Jim Toepfer; infield, Donald Peckham.

In addition to the veteran submarine hurler, Friedl Anders, Coach Guy Throner, '14, is pinning his mound hopes on sophomore Bob Houser and freshman Arthur Hug.

There was no southern trip this year, because of war economy measures, and there hasn't been much spring-time weather for outdoor practice. Here's the schedule:

April 17—Ohio Wesleyan at Delaware
April 24—Kenyon at Oberlin
April 27—Camp Perry at Oberlin*
May 1—DePauw at Greencastle
May 6—Ohio State at Oberlin*
May 8—Wooster at Wooster*
May 15—Bowling Green at Oberlin
May 22—Kent State at Oberlin
*One game. All other dates are double headers.

Kinseymen Will Have Tough Going to Repeat Conference Victory

Coach Dan Kinsey has heavy work ahead this spring to defend his Conference championship honors. Point getters for 36½ of last year's total of 45½ were lost by graduation.

Remaining are only three Yeomen who scored in the annual classic: Captain Paul Nelson, fifth in the mile; Eaton Freeman and Wyatt Miller, second and third respectively in the 2-mile.

Stars conspicuous by their absence are Jack Orebaugh, Dave Hildner, Herb Hansen, Tom Wood, Bob DeGroff, Bob Dew and others.

In addition to the above three returning lettermen, Kinsey will have Allen Arnold in the shot put and discus; Grant Chave, who high jumped 6' in the indoor K. of C. meet in Cleveland a month ago; Harry Hamilton, hurdler and jumper; and Fred Trezise, who ran one leg in the winning mile relay of a year ago.

One of the brightest prospects among the newcomers is Lloyd Duff, sophomore from Lakewood, who placed second in the high hurdles and tied for first in the pole vault at 12' 6" in the State High School Meet at Columbus last spring. His best time of 14.7 seconds in the high hurdles stamps him as a potential Conference champion in that event.

In practice sessions, outstanding in the dashes have been Charles Redmond and Joel Hayden. In the quarter-mile: Beverly Dorsey, Fred Trezise and Anthony Terepka. Roy Knipper and Robert Paul lead the half-mile candidates. In the distance events, Captain Paul Nelson, Wyatt Miller and Eaton Freeman are tops.

Outstanding among the hurdlers are Lloyd Duff, Harry Hamilton, Joel Hayden and Ellis Scott. Duff, Hamilton and Hayden are also Kinsey's chief pole vaulting hopes. In the high jump are Chave, Dick Hacker, Hamilton and Duff. Five broad jumpers are in the 20-foot class: Hayden, Bill Moore, Duff, Hamilton and Redmond. The shot put and discus candidates include, in addition to Arnold, Halsey Gulick, Bill Robertson and Hamilton.

The Yeoman thinclads will open their 1943 schedule at Baldwin-Wallace on April 28th. May 1 will find the Scots from Wooster invading the Oberlin campus. Case is scheduled on the home card for May 6 and Carnegie Tech tentatively on May 22. The Kinseymen will travel to Ohio Wesleyan on May 11 and to the Ohio Conference Track and Field Meet to be held at Berea on May 15.

Only Two Lettermen Remain On Butler's Tennis Squad

Only two lettermen remain from last year's tennis team which was undefeated in dual competition; Wilbur Euerle and Charles Redmond. The number one and two men, Dick LeFevre and Herb Hansen graduated, and the next three, Captain-elect Clint Doggett, Shelly Wolin and Don Pfeifer are in the service.

Although prospects are not bright for a season duplicating last year's, Coach Butler has about thirty candidates battling for the top six spots on the varsity ladder which will constitute the team.

The schedule:

April 22—Wooster at Oberlin
April 27—Ohio Wesleyan at Delaware
April 29—Wooster at Wooster
May 8—Ohio Wesleyan at Oberlin
May 12—Otterbein at Oberlin
May 15—Conference Championships at Kenyon
May 18—Otterbein at Westerville
May 22—Carnegie Tech at Oberlin

Golf Champions Start Their Season April 30

Only one member of Oberlin's Ohio Conference championship golf team is back this year, so the coming season is a question mark.

Captain Bob Drummond, Number two man on last year's team, is the only returning letterman. John Carlisle and Dick Holmes graduated and Don Becker, the number four man, is in the service.

Other candidates for the team include Bob Schloerb and Bob Wiltsie, both basketball lettermen, and Wesley Greider, Walter Haas, Arthur Harrow and Hal Oliver.

As Wooster and Oberlin are the only schools in the conference sponsoring golf this spring, the annual tournament has been cancelled and only two matches with the Scots have been scheduled to date: April 30 at Wooster, and a return match at Oberlin on May 7.

Wartime Physical Training Demonstrated During Intramural Festival

Oberlin's Fifteenth Annual Intramural Festival took place at the scheduled time early in March and assumed a totally new appearance. Its theme was a "War-Time Festival" with emphasis on the Physical Fitness program now being given in Physical Education Classes.

There were Ranger Calisthenics, taken from the official Navy Pre-flight Physical Training manual. The Commando Race was an indoor adaptation of the outdoor Commando Course. Relays and combative games by the freshman physical education classes, an exhibition by the tumbling and apparatus group under L. M. Bollinger, '44' of Lansdale, Pennsylvania, and the house championship basketball game between Beacon and South Noah, with Beacon the winner, made up the rest of the program.

One of the more important changes was in having large groups perform rather than individuals. The only exception to this was a last minute addition to the program, a table tennis exhibition by Albert Warner, '46' state champion of Colorado and Wyoming, and Roy Whitman, '45' second ranking junior champion in the United States, and champion in Connecticut, Pennsylvania and New York.

Oberlin Was Well Represented At National Physical Education Meeting

Oberlin was well represented at the 48th annual convention of the American Association for Health, Physical Education and Recreation which met in Cincinnati, from April 13 to 16. Dr. Jay B. Nash, '11' Professor of Physical Education at New York University, is president of the Association for 1943.

Tracy Strong, '08' was a principal speaker, discussing his work for the relief of the prisoners of war of all nations. Other Oberlinites who were principals on the program were:

Dr. Hubert C. Herring, '11, who discussed "The Promise of Pan Americanism"; Colonel M. Thomas Tchou, a resident of Oberlin and former member of the staff of Generalissimo Chiang Kaishek; Dr. Jesse F. Williams, '09, Visiting Professor of Physical Education at the University of North Carolina; and Lieutenant Commander T. Nelson Metcalf, '12' of the U. S. Navy.

Various members of the Oberlin departments of physical education were prominent in the round table conferences.

WINFRED HANNS (FRIEDL) ANDERS, '43
... the veteran submarine ball hurler on whom Coach Guy Throner, '14' pins much of his hopes for a successful baseball season. Friedl, a geography major, is a member of the U. S. Army Reserve Corps Unassigned under orders to finish up his final term in College. All recent Oberlin grads remember his peculiar but effective underslung delivery.

Under the Elms

(Continued from Page 9)

Special Permission Granted for Students' Wartime Weddings

During the month of March, four women from the senior class, with permission from college authorities, were married and then returned to school to finish up their college work and graduate in June.

Helen Humbert and Ensign John Bartow, '42' were married March 27 in Marble Collegiate Church, New York City; Dorothy Walker and Ensign Richard Crellin, a graduate of Lafayette College, were married in Canaan, New York, on March 27; Martha Finzer and Pvt. Thomas A. Leathers were married on March 26 in Apple Creek, Ohio; and Florence Roof became Mrs. Robert Allen Krieger on March 12. She was married at South Sterling, Pennsylvania. Several other senior women will marry men in service at Commencement time.

Daughters of Alumni Make Phi Beta Kappa and Honors Lists

When the names of Phi Beta Kappa members for the graduating class and honor students for the freshmen class were announced on April 6, the names

of four students who are daughters of alumni were read.

Eleanor Cady, daughter of Dr. (t. '16) and Mrs. Lyman Cady (Muriel E. Poor, '16) was elected to membership in Phi Beta Kappa.

Phyllis Ann Brockman, daughter of Mr. and Mrs. A. D. Brockmann, (Joyce Eckhart, '18) was in the highest quarter of those seniors graduating from the Conservatory of Music with the degree of Bachelor of Music Education.

On the freshman honor list were Catherine Fauver, daughter of the late Richard R. Fauver, '17' and Mrs. Fauver and Martha Vogt, daughter of Mr. ('17) and Mrs. W. W. Vogt (Nellie V. Renneckar, con '18).

Junior Girl Wins Class of '15 Oratorical Contest

Jane Crowe, junior from Lakewood, and Daniel Reddin, senior from North Baltimore, Ohio, were winners Monday evening, April 12, in the annual class of 1915 oratorical contest.

Miss Crowe, who placed first, won $60 with her speech on "The Need for International Organization." Mr. Reddin placed second and won $40 with his address on "Development of Airways in the Future."

The Class of 1915 Prize Contests are

an annual affair. The speeches given in the oratorical contest must be original and may deal with any subject in the field of public affairs.

On Friday evening, April 16, the prize debate was held. The teams competing debated the question "Should the United Nations establish a permanent federal union with powers to tax, to regulate international commerce, and to maintain an international police force?"

Members of the winning team which received a prize of $150 to be divided evenly among the members, were, Wesley Brashares, junior from Ann Arbor, Jane Crowe and Fay Calkins, senior from Arlington, Virginia.

The prizes for this contest are made possible by a gift from a member of the class of 1915, who prefers to remain anonymous.

Taxi Dance—Leap Year Style— Sells $130 in War Stamps

A new version of the taxi dance, with men acting as "hostesses" and women buying war savings stamps to dance with them, sold $130 in war savings stamps within two hours on Friday evening, April 16. The dance was sponsored by the Victory Through Action Committee.

Men students and faculty members were "hostesses." Women paid a ten cent war stamp for one dance, twenty-five cent stamp for three dances.

In order to eliminate for the women the embarrassment of having to ask men to dance, the "hostesses" left the floor after each dance and lined up behind two screens, tall men behind one, short men behind the other. The women, likewise, formed two lines, according to height; upon presenting a ticket which indicated she had bought a stamp, the purchaser danced away with the man who appeared from behind the screen. Music was furnished by the all-girl dance band, members of which donated their services.

Students are clamoring for another taxi dance, at which men and women will take turn about being hostesses.

Moyer to Washington

Raymond T. Moyer, '21, has taken a position as Senior Agriculturist in the Department of Agriculture, Office of Foreign Agricultural Relations, Washington, D. C. His work will have to do with relations with China and, at the beginning, will consist in the gathering of information related to a possible granting of Agricultural Aid to that country. Mrs. Moyer and daughters, Susan, Joan, and Ann will join him after June 1.

WITH THE FACULTY

Lewis and Lockwood Win Guggenheim Fellowships

Professors J. D. Lewis and Normand Lockwood were among the seven Ohioans who received Guggenheim fellowships this year, it was announced Monday, March 29.

The John Simon Guggenheim Memorial Foundation grants fellowships annually to creative workers in all fields who "by their previous work have shown themselves to be persons of unusual ability." The stipends average about $2,500.

Dr. Lewis, associate professor of political science, received his fellowship to work on the preparation of a book on trends in American political thought and institutions since 1900.

Professor Lockwood's grant was made "for creative work in musical composition."

Both men will receive leaves of absence for next year in order to take advantage of the fellowships, although neither has completed definite plans for that time. Professor Lewis expects to spend a year in a place convenient to a large library, possibly at Harvard or Columbia. Professor Lockwood will probably spend the year in New York City.

In all, 11 women and 53 men received awards this year.

Economists to Aid Colombia

Ben W. Lewis, professor of economics now on leave on Government service, and James R. Nelson, '36, former instructor of economics, have gone to Bogora, Colombia, to help officials of the Colombian government work out an anti-inflation program.

Lewis, special assistant to the CPA Deputy Administrator for Prices, and Nelson, economist in the export and import branch of the agency, will advise with a price control committee now being set up in Colombia.

Faculty Briefs

Professor H. H. Thornton of the Department of Romance Languages, made two addresses in Cleveland late in March. He spoke at Laurel School and before the Italian Literary Club of Cleveland.

Professor Howard Robinson, head of the History Department, has received a Grant-in-Aid from the Social Science Research Council in order to complete his *"History of the British Post Office."*

JOHN D. LEWIS, '28
. . . preparing a book on trends in American political thought and institutions since 1900

Dr. R. W. Wagner, lieutenant, j. g. in the U. S. Navy, instructor in mathematics now on leave from the college, has had an article entitled "Differentials and Analytic Continuation in Commutative Algebras" published in the *Duke Mathematical Journal* for December, 1942. Lt. Wagner is at present an instructor in mathematics at Annapolis.

President E. H. Wilkins was in Columbus April 2-3, for his final duties as President of the Ohio College Association for the year 1942-43. He presided at a meeting of the Executive Committee of the Association and at the annual business meeting of the Association. The usual three-day Spring meeting of the Association was omitted because of travel conditions.

President Wilkins has been asked by the Navy to serve as a member of the final Board of Review for V-12 applicants in this region. The Board will consist of three members, of whom one will be a Naval officer and the other two civilians.

Professor Leo C. Holden, now on sabbatical leave from the conservatory, is studying with Carl Weinrich, organist at Columbia and Princeton Universities. On April 18, Mr. Holden played for the St. John's Passion, by Bach, in Princeton, N. J. His address is 540 West 122nd St., New York.

Professor Chester L. Shaver is the author of two articles which have appeared in recent publications. One is entitled "Philemon, Physician" published in the Annals of Medical History for November, 1942; the other entitled "Chaucer's Owls and Apes" appeared in Modern Language Notes, February 1943.

Professor Walter Horton returned to Oberlin in February from St. Petersburg, Florida, where he had gone for rest following a severe illness. He has resumed his classes in the Graduate School of Theology.

Robert Clark, instructor in physical education, and coach of the varsity basketball team, has been commissioned an ensign in the U. S. Naval Reserve. On March 18 he reported at the University of North Carolina, Chapel Hill, for a one-month training period.

Following training he will be an instructor of physical education in a Navy pre-flight school. He has been granted leave of absence from the college.

Associate Professor Fred Foreman has received an honorable discharge from the U. S. Army and has returned to the Oberlin faculty to aid in instructing the Navy V-12 unit.

M RS. WALTER H. MERRIAM, a former member of the Oberlin College Board of Trustees, died on March 19 at her home in Hollywood, California.

Mrs. Merriam was the former Cliffe Johnson, daughter of the late Albert B. Johnson, Oberlin banker, who also served as a member of the college's board of trustees. She studied in the College and Conservatory with the class of 1889 and graduated from Cleveland Medical College in 1895, though she never actively practiced medicine.

During her many years of residence in Cleveland, Mrs. Merriam was active in the work of the Y. W. C. A. and the Phillis Wheatley Association and was the first woman elected to the Cleveland Community Fund Council.

Following her death the Cleveland *Plain Dealer*, in an editorial headed "A Noblewoman Passes," spoke of Mrs. Merriam as follows:

"Of comparatively few persons can it be said so truly as it can be said of Mrs. Walter H. Merriam that she lived primarily to make the world a better place for others. From early girlhood until her death at the age of 76, the ruling passion of her life was the welfare of those less fortunate than herself.

MRS. CLIFFE JOHNSON MERRIAM, x'89
. . . a noblewoman in the truest sense of the word

"The forces for social betterment which she set in motion during her many happy and active years in Cleveland will continue to grow and produce rich harvests long after her name is gone from the lips and memories of the beneficiaries. Mrs. Merriam was a noblewoman in the truest sense of the word."

She is survived by her brother Albert M. Johnson.

D R. HERBERT ALDEN YOUTZ, emeritus professor of Philosophy of Religion and Christian Ethics in the Oberlin Graduate School of Theology, died in Springfield, Massachusetts, March 20, after a severe illness of several months.

Professor Youtz retired in 1932 after fourteen years of teaching in Oberlin. He was born April 28, 1867, on a farm near Des Moines, Iowa, the eldest son of Hiram L. and Caroline Preston Youtz, and graduated in 1890 from Simpson College, Indianola, Iowa. Receiving the S.T.B. degree in 1895 at Boston University, he preached in Congregational churches in East Dennis and Quincy, Massachusetts, and later in Middlefield in the Berkshires where he was ordained in 1897. He served only one other pastorate, in East Providence, Rhode Island (1899-1901), following which he studied abroad on a fellowship from Boston University for two years at the Universities at Marburg and Berlin. He completed his Doctorate in Philosophy at Boston in 1904, where he had also won his Phi Beta Kappa membership.

There followed his three decades of theological teaching and writing, with an increasing success which was recognized by his final honorary degree of Doctor of Theology (S.T.D.), conferred by his Boston alma mater.

During an interim in pastorates at the Second Church in Oberlin Doctor Youtz served with marked acceptance as pulpit supply for some weeks. His preaching is remembered as notably concise, pointed, challenging, needing nothing of the ornate to make it winsome, and lacking nothing of clarity to win confidence in the truth of his convictions.

Dr. Youtz taught at the Chicago Theological Seminary, McGill University and Auburn Theological Seminary, and came to Oberlin in 1918.

One of his Oberlin colleagues and intimate friends, Professor G. Walter Fiske, has written as follows in tribute to Dr. Youtz.

"He is gratefully remembered as a gracious gentleman of quiet dignity, broad scholarship, and real insight into life's meanings and values. As a philosopher he was a thorough-going Idealist, one of the ablest disciples of the beloved Doctor Bowen of Boston, and taught 'personalism' with an enthusiasm born of deep conviction. His appreciative students were inspired by his loyalty to 'The Supremacy of the Spiritual,' the fine title of his greatest book, published early in his Oberlin career.

"Herbert Youtz' appreciation of the beautiful was as keen as his quest for truth.

"In nothing is the rare fineness of his spirit and his luminous mind more clearly evident than in his poems. Many of his friends felt his true poetic insight, though he left but a few published poems—just a lovely bit of verse now and then to share his vision through some periodical. His deep love for Oberlin we find recorded in one lilting Oberlin song, and more notably in his beautiful lines to Alma Mater, interpreting the inner meaning of Kenyon Cox's symbolism in his superb mural lunettes in the east entrance to the Administration Building. These, reproduced in color, made more luminous by Herbert Youtz' verses, were published some years ago by the College."

Two of Professor Youtz' family hold Oberlin degrees, his son Philip, '19, of Washington, D. C., and his daughter Julia, '23, now Mrs. Emil Andersen of Springfield, Massachusetts, where Mrs. Mary Newell Youtz, so well remembered in Oberlin, also survives him, as a winter resident in the Sheraton Hotel.

The funeral service on March 22d was conducted by a former Oberlin student, Dr. H. H. Deck, of Springfield,

ALUMNI CLUB NEWS

Ruth Armstrong Leppmann Is New President in Chicago

The annual business meeting of the *Oberlin Women's Club of Chicago* was held Saturday afternoon, April 10, in Chicago's Boy Scout Headquarters, Mrs. Edward J. F. Young (Helen Templeton, '26) presiding. By a fortunate coincidence J. E. Wirkler, who was in town interviewing high school students managed to find time to attend the meeting and brought latest news from the campus.

The report of the treasurer showed a balance of more than $300 and no time was lost in voting that amount to the scholarship fund of Oberlin College.

The following officers were elected: President, Mrs. Ruth Armstrong Leppmann, '37; first vice-president, Mrs. Dorothy Bracken Pettijohn, '28; second vice-president, Margaret Jacobs, '39; treasurer, Mrs. Laura Schwahn Whitney, x'26; assistant treasurer, Ruth Vehe, '37; recording secretary, Mary Hoppe, '40; corresponding secretary, Mrs. Laura Shurtleff Price, '93; councillor to Oberlin Alumni Council, Mrs. Marie Radcliff Lauthers, '21·

North Shore Woman's Club

Mrs. Emmons Coe opened her home in Evanston, Illinois, for a dessert-luncheon for the *North Shore Oberlin Woman's Club* on March 12. Mrs. N. Conner Gunn, (Mary McFarland k'25) was the assisting hostess.

Miss Barbara Malott, coloratura soprano, presented a musical program accompanied by her mother, Mrs. Herman F. Malott, (Irene Cox, '08). Lieutenant Hartley, a WAVE from the office of procurement in Chicago, spoke informally concerning the women's reserve of the Navy.

Dorothy Hayford Watkins of Pittsburgh To Be New Assistant Dean

The Oberlin College Alumni Association of Pittsburgh held its final meeting of the year, the Annual Spring Banquet, on April 13 at the College Club of Pittsburgh. The meeting was well attended by some 65 members. Mrs. Birger Engstrom, president, presided at the short business meeting which followed the dinner. The business activities, treasurer's report, and social events of the year were reviewed. We are especially proud of the year book, an Alumni Directory, which we had published this year.

Elections for the coming year were held, with these results: President, Mrs. Birger Engstrom '18; Vice-president, Mrs. Louise Wakefield Erler, '32; Secretary, Barbara J. King, '41; Treasurer, Dr. Elbert M. Shelton, '17; Social Chairman, Mrs. Eleanor Cunningham Slease, '38; Alumni Counselor, Mrs. Ruth Anderegg Frost, '13·

After the business meeting, President Wilkins spoke about Oberlin today and how she is meeting the present war situation. We were especially interested in hearing about the details concerning the incoming Navy V-12 unit.

President Wilkins also surprised us by announcing the appointment of our present social chairman, Mrs. Thomas A. (Dorothy Hayford '38) Watkins as new assistant dean of women. The meeting ended with hearty singing of Oberlin songs.

Commander McAfee and Professor Jelliffe Address New York Alumni

The New York Club held a highly successful dinner meeting at the Town Hall Club on the evening of April 6. Of the 170 in attendance many were in the uniforms of the various armed services.

Carlton K. Matson, '15· president of the club presided as toastmaster. The program was introduced with the singing of several tenor solos by Tom Edwards, '38· who was accompanied by his wife, Eleanor Zellers Edwards, '39· Lieutenant Commander Mildred A. McAfee, h'39, was the principal speaker giving a most interesting picture of what she considered might be the effect of the war on the liberal arts colleges. She also told several amusing incidents in the early days of WAVES organization which she commands.

Other speakers were Professor R. A. Jelliffe who talked about changes which have occurred on the campus as a result of the war, and about plans for the Navy V-12 Unit. Alumni Secretary Thomas Harris reported on the activities of the Association.

After a rising vote of appreciation extended to President Wilkins for the fine program he is maintaining for keeping in touch with the men in service, the nominating committee's report was read by Maurice Merryfield, '30· and new officers were elected. Names of the new officers will be obtained for publication next month.

Southern Californians Hear Col. M. Thomas Tchou

Thirty-eight members and friends of the *Southern California Oberlin Alumni Association* met for dinner March 30 at the Martha Washington Tea Rooms, Los Angeles. The meeting was in honor of Colonel M. Thomas Tchou of Oberlin, director of the World Citizenship Movement and former member of Generalissimo Chiang Kai-shek's official family.

Colonel Tchou was introduced by Mrs. Lucy Rice Winkler, '18· He addressed the group on the World Citizenship Movement.

Sixty-Five Attend Cincinnati Luncheon on April 14

More than 65 alumni gathered at the Hotel Gibson in Cincinnati on April 14, for a luncheon meeting. Many of those present were attending the National War Fitness Conference of the American Health, Physical Education, and Recreation Association.

Short talks were given by Lieutenant Commander T. Nelson Metcalf, '12· Tracy Strong, '08· Joel Haydn, '09, C. W. Savage, '93· John G. Olmstead, '06, Gertrude Moulton, '03· and J. Herbert Nichols, '11·

Arrangements for the luncheon were made by Mary Cochran, '03·

Boston Alumni Reelect Woodruff

The *Boston Chapter of the Alumni Association* held its annual dinner on April 13 in the Women's Republican Club. More than 60 alumni and friends attended. For the coming year President John R. Woodruff, '33· was re-elected, and Louis D. Gibbs, '98· was chosen secretary.

Dr. W. Frederick Bohn gave a highlight review of Oberlin as he has known it in his 38 years of service to the College, closing his talk with the announcement of the plans for the Navy V-12 Unit. Alumni Secretary Harris told of the work of the Association and the plans for this year's Alumni Fund.

Oberlin Alumni Enjoy Supper Together in Cincinnati

A supper get-together, arranged by Professors George E. Waln, Marian S. Williams, and Arthur L. Williams, all of the Conservatory faculty, was held on Sunday evening, March 28, at Canary Cottage in Cincinnati, Ohio, for former students and alumni of Oberlin attending the North Central Music-in-Wartime Institute. The Institute, sponsored by the North Central Music Educators Conference, included representatives from ten states.

S

After the business meeting, President Wilkins spoke about Oberlin today and how she is meeting the present war situation. We were especially interested in hearing about the details concerning the incoming Navy V-12 unit.

President Wilkins also surprised us by announcing the appointment of our present social chairman, Mrs. Thomas A. (Dorothy Hayford '38) Watkins as new assistant dean of women. The meeting ended with hearty singing of Oberlin songs.

Commander McAfee and Professor Jelliffe Address New York Alumni

The New York Club held a highly successful dinner meeting at the Town Hall Club on the evening of April 6. Of the 170 in attendance many were in the uniforms of the various armed services.

Carlton K. Matson, '15, president of the club presided as toastmaster. The program was introduced with the singing of several tenor solos by Tom Edwards, '38, who was accompanied by his wife, Eleanor Zellers Edwards, '39. Lieutenant Commander Mildred A. McAfee, h'39, was the principal speaker giving a most interesting picture of what she considered might be the effect of the war on the liberal arts colleges. She also told several amusing incidents in the early days of WAVES organization which she commands.

Other speakers were Professor R. A. Jelliffe who talked about changes which have occurred on the campus as a result of the war, and about plans for the Navy V-12 Unit. Alumni Secretary Thomas Harris reported on the activities of the Association.

After a rising vote of appreciation to President Wilkins for the program he is maintaining for the men in service, ... in touch with the men in service... ...earing committee's report, '30, ... e Merryfield... ...red.... ...for

Southern Californians Hear Col. M. Thomas Tchou

Thirty-eight members and five friends of the Southern California Oberlin Club met at the Martha Washington Hotel, 30 at the Martha Washington Hotel, Los Angeles. The meeting was in honor of Colonel M. Thomas Tchou of Oberlin, director of the World Citizenship Movement and former member of Generalissimo Chiang Kai-shek's official family.

Colonel Tchou was introduced by Mrs. Lucy Rice Winkler, '18. He addressed the group on the World Citizenship Movement.

Sixty-Five Attend Cincinnati Luncheon on April 14

More than 65 alumni gathered at the Hotel Gibson in Cincinnati on April 14, for a luncheon meeting. Many of those present were attending the National War Fitness Conference of the American Health, Physical Education and Recreation Association.

Short talks were given by Lieutenant Commander T. Nelson Metcalf, '12, Tracy Strong, '08, Joel Hayda, '69, C. W. Savage, '93, John G. Olmsted, '94, Gertrude Moulton, '03, and J. Herbert Nichols, '11.

Arrangements for the luncheon were made by Mary Cochran, '08.

Boston Alumni Reelect Woodruff

The Boston Chapter of the Alumni Association held its annual dinner on April 13 in the Women's Republican Club. More than 60 alumni and friends attended. For the coming year President John R. Woodruff, '33, was reelected, and Louis D. Gibbs, '98, was chosen secretary.

Dr. W. Frederick Bohn gave a high-light review of Oberlin as he has known it in his 38 years of service at the College, closing his talk with the announcement of the plans for the Navy V-12 Unit. Alumni Secretary Harris told of the work of the Association and the plans for this year's Alumni Fund.

Oberlin Alumni Enjoy Supper Together in Cincinnati

A supper get-together, arranged by Professors George E. Wells, Martin J. Williams, and Arthur L. Williams, all of the Conservatory, March 28, at Cincinnati. On Sunday evening, March 28, at Cincinnati Cottage on Alumni of Oberlin Conservatory students and alumni of Oberlin former students and Central Music students attending the National Music Educators Institute. The Institute sponsored by the North Central Music Educators Conference, included representatives from ten states.

"TEN THOUSAND STRONG

Edited by Rebecca Bright

Academy

James L. Stone, Acad. '02-'03, is president and general manager of the Danbury and Bethel Gas and Electric Light Company of Danbury, Connecticut. He was located in the West for a number of years, and in 1928 was president of the Spokane, Washington, Chamber of Commerce.

1884

The Reverend Clarence A. Vincent, (t'88) died March 31 at his home on the shore of Virginia Lake, in Winter Park, Florida.

Mr. Vincent was born eighty-four years ago at Bainbridge, Ohio. He took post graduate work at Yale after receiving his B. D. degree at Oberlin, and in 1898 he received the honorary D. D. degree from Hillsdale College. He served many pastorates in his lifetime, including churches at Buffalo, Boston, and Washington, D. C. He was active in various organizations, having been president of Congregational State Associations in Ohio, Illinois, and Florida; president of the World's Scientific Association; and president of the Hungerford Industrial School.

He was pastor at Winter Park for seventeen years and had transformed the village frame building used as the church into the present fine edifice of brick and stone. He was a powerful factor in community interests and owned and operated a large orange grove.

Mr. Vincent is survived by his wife, the former Lucy S. Hall, '85-'89; three daughters, Hope, '11, Ruth E., and Helen (Mrs. Franklin C. McLean); and three sons, Clarence H. '20, Donald C., x'25, and Howard F., '26.

1878

Ella Chambers Bassett died March 15 at her home, 14608 Strathmore Ave., East Cleveland. She was the widow of the late Charles M. Bassett who died 20 years ago. Surviving are two daughters, Mrs. R. C. Almy and Mrs. E. J. Benson, and two sons, Edward W. Bassett and R. M. Bassett.

1891

Willard L. Beard, see 1928.

1894

Artemus E. Bullock, Con., has made his home in Iowa Falls, Iowa, most of his life. He has been director of the Ellsworth Conservatory of Music since 1903. Mr. Bullock has also taught music in New York City and this past year in Chicago.

A radio broadcast in March from E. S. Turner, A. M. '31, who has been interned by the Japanese since the fall of Manila, came by short wave from the radio station at Tokio. It states that all Y. M. C. A. secretaries and their families including Mr. and Mrs. Bertram E. Merriam (O. C. '94) are safe and well and that several, including the Turners and Merriams, had been released in January from Santa Thomas University where they had been interned.

A newspaper clipping of the Tokio broadcast was forwarded to Oberlin from Grinnell, Iowa, by Mrs. Louise Hill Norton, who was visiting her daughter, Mrs. Ralph Noyce, in Grinnell.

Mrs. Fred P. Loomis (Mary Rodgers) was reported to be seriously ill in March at her home in Omaha.

1898

Miss Eva Jane Smith, Con., died on March 22, at her home in Warren, Pennsylvania.

She was the daughter of Levi Smith, a wealthy industrialist of Warren who in his life-time gave largely to Warren institutions and to foreign missions.

Miss Smith had travelled extensively, especially in the orient in her later years, and had made a particular study in Singapore and Calcutta of Eastern thought. She had allied her-

self with movements of spiritual philosophy in France and England. Returning to America in 1933, she disseminated, at her own expense, leaflets embodying the meditations of leaders of the group as well as guides for daily living of her own composition. She also contributed poems to various periodicals. Ever forward looking, she was a pioneer in the Woman's Suffrage movement, belonging to four Pennsylvania organizations and becoming a captain in the York unit.

Her death is a great loss to those who knew her fine qualities and enjoyed her staunch and loyal friendship.

—Helen T. French

1899

David Carroll Churchill returned to Dayton, Kentucky, in March from an observation trip to Alaska for the U. S. Army Air Forces. He was engaged in designing and inventing various devices to make fighting planes more reliable and efficient especially in cold weather, and is working at Wright Field, Dayton, Ohio. He recently wrote that the Alaskan trip "was delightful because novel, but pretty strenuous for an old man."

1901

Charlene Sperry teaches in the high school at Des Moines, Iowa, and spends her summers at her cottage on Puget Sound, Seattle. Her address in Des Moines is 937-38th St.

Althea Rowland Woodruff (Mrs. C. M.) is teaching lip-reading in the Adult Education department of Los Angeles County public school system three days a week. She does volunteer work in education in Residual Hearing at the Tracy Clinic on other days. Her home address is 1064½ Ashton Ave.

Mrs. Edgar H. Price (Anna Morton) teaches at her home in Long Beach, California.

Edwin Brouse reports that his son, Robert, is an ensign in the Navy, stationed at present at the Naval Officers' Procurement Office, Rochester, New York. His daughter, Mary, is a junior at Oberlin.

Virginia Billings, who is still living in Tempe, Arizona, took a trip to Mexico City last year.

Jennie Gurwell Niederhauser (Mrs. Sam W.) writes from San Diego, California, that she has three grandchildren. Her son, Robert, bought a 70 acre ranch and is building a home there in his spare time.

W. Moreton Owen, who lives on Ellsworth Road, Waterbury, Connecticut, has recently completed a booklet of 116 mimeographed pages entitled, "Mary Benedict Owen—The Story of a Devoted Life," dedicated to his wife who died in 1939.

1902

Mrs. Smythe, wife of Burns Smythe, Con., '01, died last fall. This winter Mr. Smythe has been visiting his son, Mark, at Palm Beach, Florida, and his son, Charles, at Cleveland, His present address is 1475 Virginia Way, La Jolla, California.

Mr. '03, and Mrs. Allan Lightner (Helen Chute) had as their guest in Waterville, Maine, in February, Keyes O. Metcalf, '11, librarian of Harvard University and president of the American Library Association. Mr. Metcalf spoke at a meeting of the Colby College Library Associates on "The Value of Collections of Letters."

1903

Myra Myrick spent the winter in Tucson, Arizona. She spent her time studying Spanish and working for the Red Cross.

Della Purcell Harding—See class of 1933.

1904

Harry W. Bails, who has been very ill, is now in Coconut Grove, Florida, and is anxious to hear from his Oberlin friends.

1907

Dr. and Mrs. Roscoe Van Nuys have announced the marriage of their daughter. Marian Ellen, to John D. Frederickson. The wedding took place March 14 in San Francisco, California.

Dr. H. Waldo Spiers, orthopedic surgeon, died in Los Angeles, California, July 10, 1942, at the age of 57. He is survived by his wife, son, and daughter.

Mr. and Mrs. Wesley Frost (Priscilla Clapp) —See class of 1936.

1909

Professor George S. Dickinson was absent from his teaching at Vassar College last semester, because of a severe illness. Mrs. Dickinson (Bessie McClure) reports that her husband, after two major operations, is now completely recovered and is carrying his usual schedule of work.

Mabel Eldred has changed her New York City address. She is now living at 162 W. 54th St. Mabel tells of meeting Mrs. Russel I. Hare. (Florence Bright. '05-'09) and having a visit with her. Florence's husband has been receiving treatment for an illness at Clifton Springs. New York.

Frank R. Gott, who is principal of Lafayette High School, Buffalo, New York, reports that war activities, as well as school work, keep him pretty well occupied, and that Mrs. Gott (Cora Prefert, '12) is doing a good job at maintaining the family morale. Their daughter, Esther, '40, who received a Master's degree from the University of Rochester in 1942, is now in the editorial office of the "Buffalo Evening News." Ruth Gott, '42, is a student at a Buffalo business school, and Evelyn, the Gotts' youngest daughter, is a freshman at Oberlin, enrolled in a combination college and conservatory course. The Gott family lives at 528 E. Utica St, Buffalo.

1910

Mr. '08, and Mrs. Irving L. Fisher (Clara Taylor) have a large tourist home, "Kenka Inn," at 133 E. Rich Ave., DeLand, Florida. Oberlin friends visiting Florida will be heartily welcome. The Fishers' two sons are married and live in New York State. Edward, who is with Bell Aircraft in Buffalo, has a son, Ronald Edward. Robert, who works for Dupont at Niagara Falls, has a daughter, Sharon Joye.

Mrs. James L. Graham (Dorothy Fairchild) writes that her husband is acting head of the department of psychology at Lehigh University. She says they are doing the "usual" things. Dorothy is president of the local branch of the A. A. U. W. Their daughter graduates from junior high this year. And a victory garden to rival last year's excellent one is already planned. Dorothy's father, James Thome Fairchild, '83, lives with them.

Mrs. Colin M. Higgins (Edith Ballou) reports that she is doing volunteer service with the rationing board, giving lectures on current literature and creative writing, and is teaching a group on the latter subject. Her daughter, Anne, is very happy as a freshman at Oberlin. Her son, Allen, is a Naval Air Cadet, and her son, Colin, is in C. A. A. Administration in Washington.

Ralph W. Kerr is a chemist with the Unitcast Corporation, Toledo, a company engaged one hundred per cent in war work. He and Mrs. Kerr have two grandchildren, Donald Leroy Seaman, son of their daughter Marian, and Donna Jeanne Kerr, daughter of their son, Donald Ralph. "Rusty" urges 1910ers and others to write him at 2428 Fulton St., Toledo.

Grace Leadingham is still teaching school in Los Angeles and lives at 3022 Shrine Place. She writes, "I have attained what might well be the dearest wish of certain millions of the world's inhabitants in that I go along day by day with absolutely nothing spectacular to relate."

Mr. and Mrs. Bayard Lyon (Elsie Chung), who formerly made their home in Daytona Beach, Florida, have accepted a position in Chicago with the Wilson-Jones Company, manufacturers and wholesalers of looseleaf devices and stationery. Their new address is 431 N. Drake Ave.

Mrs. Paul P. MacCollin (Elizabeth F. Newton, Con.) of Sioux City, Iowa, writes, "Paul and I are at the same place we started in so long ago. Our 16 year old daughter is in high

ACCLAIMED not only at home, but in Europe and South America as well, Evangeline Lehman has won an enviable reputation as singer, composer and teacher. The picture above was taken when the Detroit Institute of Musical Art conferred upon Miss Lehman the honorary degree of Doctor of Music, in 1940.

Graduating from the Oberlin Conservatory of Music in 1919, Miss Lehman first became known as a teacher and recitalist in the Middlewest.

In 1931 she won honors at the American Conservatory of Fontainebleau and during her residence in France she gained distinction as the contralto soloist at the American Cathedral in Paris, and was also active as a vocal coach. Several distinguished French singers, including Mme. Doniau-Blanc, of the Opera, Mme. Magdeleine Gresle, and others came under her instruction. Her talent brought her the praise and friendship of such musical notables as Isidor Philipp, Maurice Dumesnil, Marcel Dupre, Maurice Ravel and others. For her work as a composer and singer she was honored by the French Government, in 1933, with a special Medal of the Ministers des Affaires Etrangeres which she received from the hands of the great musiciain, Charles-Marie Widor. She also was awarded the Palms of an Officer of the French Academy.

Miss Lehman's first publications were issued in 1932. They are now featured on programs the country over, and continue their appeal to a constantly growing audience. Best known perhaps is her religious oratorio "Sainte Thérèse of the Child Jesus" which has been performed by many of the finest choruses

EVANGELINE LEHMAN, '19
... thrice talented, honored at home and abroad as singer, composer and teacher.

and orchestras in Europe and throughout this hemisphere. The Ruth St. Dennis ballet has performed her cantata "Noel." She has composed a number of delightful songs for children.

Miss Lehman is the wife of the internationally known French pianist, conductor and author, Maurice Dumesnil. Her home is in Highland Park, Michigan.

school. We are trying to do our bit for our country and keep as cheerful as possible during these trying times."

The death of Nell Ericson Minty on October 25, 1942, is reported by her husband, George E. Minty. Mr. Minty's address is 529 Brooks, Missoula, Montana.

Genevieve North writes from Piqua, Ohio, that she is still teaching English in high school and is active in church, club and civic organizations.

Anna B. Osborn has recently moved to 1460 Waterbury Rd., Cleveland. She is serving her fourth year as an assistant principal of Lincoln High School, Cleveland.

O. Mark Richards was recently reelected for the fifth time president of the Y. M. C. A. at Warren, Ohio. His son, Walter, '37, was elected a member of the board of trustees.

1911

Bruce Smith writes that he has joined the Civilian Personnel of the U. S. Army Air Corps, Property Section. He is stationed at the Buffalo plant of the Bell Aircraft Corporation, and since he and Mrs. Swift (Martha Storrs, '00) are living in Kenmore, New York, that means "breakfast before sun-up."

Dr. L. M. Isaacs—See class of 1940.

Mrs. Harold J. Leonard (Marian Slater)— See class of 1942.

1912

E. Stanley Grant is an enthusiastic director of the Rochdale Institute of New York City, the national training school for leaders of the consumer cooperative movement. He became a charter member of its board in 1937. Pointing to the important part cooperatives have had in keeping the Chinese nation in the fight, he writes that, though as an Oberlin student he had no interest in "foreign missions," he now thinks "perhaps consumer cooperatives, locally and internationally, are just a new form of expression of the old New England-Puritan-Oberlin missionary spirit."

1913

The many friends of Mrs. J. Morris Steck (Mary H. McCloy) will regret to learn of the death of her husband on April 17, after a brief illness, at Fredericksburg, Virginia. In addition to his widow, he leaves four children. Mr. Steck was a graduate of Gettysburg College.

1914

Helen French Isaacs, x—See class of 1940.

1918

Bill Hamilton, oldest son of Harold E. Hamilton and Palmer Lichty Bevis, elder son of Mrs. Maude Lichty Perrin, '19, are in the Army Intelligence Department with the Yale Univer-

shy Unit of the U. S. Army Air Force, in training at Miami Beach, Florida. They both hope to
be sent to the cryptology school.

Harold Hamilton is still in the Newington,
Connecticut, veterans' hospital, suffering from
a spinal difficulty incurred in World War I.
His son Bobby is a student at Mt. Hermon
school.

A letter from Sidney Bunker, '25, written in
October says that his brother Paul Bunker, left
Bombay, India, early last summer to take a responsible post with the U. S. Foreign Information Service in Delhi.

1919

Warner Berthoff, son of Nate Berthoff and
Mrs. Helen Tappan Utterback, and Bill Bevis,
second son of Mrs. Maude Lichty Perrin, both
made the headlines recently in the Hotchkiss
(School) Record. Warner starred as Stuyvesant
in "Knickerbocker Holiday" and Bill is the
newly elected Chairman of the Record.

1920

Bruce Catton, x, who has been acting as
personal spokesman for WPB Chairman Donald
M. Nelson, is now to take over as WPB information chief, succeeding Stephen E. Fitzgerald,
who becomes a deputy of Director Elmer Davis
of the OWI.

"Plain Chant for America" by William Grant
Still, Con. x, received its initial Philadelphia
performance by the Philadelphia Orchestra, under Eugene Ormandy, in March, with James
Pease, baritone, a winner of this year's Metropolitan Auditions of the Air, as soloist.

1923

Jeannette Beebe has been working as a cata-
loguer for the Cleveland Branch of the Army
Medical Library since Dec. 1, 1942, after twelve
years at Flora Stone Mather College Library
of Western Reserve. She received her M. A.
in history from Western Reserve in June, 1941.
Jeannette's address is 11209 Clifton Blvd.,
Cleveland.

Helen Harris Denny reports that her husband,
Captain William L. Denny, is serving with the
Medical Corps somewhere in England. Her fath-
er, Clyde R. Harris, died March 11

1925

Dr. and Mrs. Edgar C. Bain (Helen L. Cram)
are living at 7 Wilson Dr., Ben Avon Heights,
Pennsylvania. Dr. Bain, a member of the research staff of the United States Steel Corporation since 1928, was recently appointed vice
president of the Carnegie-Illinois Steel Company,
in charge of research and technology. He is re-
garded as one of the nation's foremost authorities on alloy steels.

A letter received recently from Sidney Bunker,
written in October, tells vividly of the effects
of the war, particularly of the fall of Singapore,
upon the affairs of his school in Vaddukoodaii,
Ceylon. He refers to the birth of his new daughter, Grace, at Wai (near Bombay), in July, and
to the fact that he and his family were then hop.
ing to leave on furlough in April, but wondered
if ship passage would be available.

1927

Mrs. Frank E. Bettridge (Leila Williams) reports that her husband is in the Army and that
she is teaching. Her address is changed to 2222
Scottwood Ave., Toledo, Ohio.

Mrs. Bourne A. Smith (Dorothy Hall) is
back at Antioch College teaching and writing
after a year on the L. L. S. Fellowship at the
University of California. Her husband is also
at Antioch working in the College Library. She
says that the Army is about to descend upon Antioch to be instructed.

Arla Wallace, Con., is still teaching choral
music in high school at McKeesport, Pennsylvania. Her address is 1008 Craig St.

Mrs. John W. Barr (Ruth Shappell, Con.)
writes from 228 E. Tammany St., Orwigsburg,
Pennsylvania, that she is still teaching school,
marking time in her life until her husband re-
turns from war. She is hoping to spend a part
of her summer vacation with him in Kansas,
if he is still in this country by then.

COMMISSIONED ENSIGNS ON APRIL 6

*. . . Betty Lee Vernon, '41, and Emma McCloy Layman, '30, were Midshipmen when
this picture was taken at Smith College*

CAPT. W. G. FENDER, x'26

*. . . escaped from Singapore to Java, he
is now in Australia*

MANAGER in Singapore for the
Goodyear Tire & Rubber Export
Company for several years, Captain
Wilbur G. Fender, x'26, joined the U.
S. Army at the time of the Japanese in-
vasion, escaped to Java, and later went
to Australia where he is now stationed.

Mr. and Mrs. Allen Latham (Ruth Nichols)
are the proud parents of a son, Thomas Walker,
born on January 18. He is their third son and
fourth child.

TWO of Oberlin's 37 women alumni
now in military uniform are pictured above as they neared the completion of their training for commissions
in the WAVES, at the U. S. Navy's
Midshipmen's School at Smith College.
They became Ensigns, USNR, on April
6. The background of the picture has
been air brushed out—some military
secret?

Miss Vernon's home is at Webster
Grove, Missouri, and she was formerly
doing secretarial work with the Rals-
ton Purina Company in St. Louis, Missouri, before entering the WAVES. She
majored in sociology at Oberlin.

Mrs. Layman, whose home is at Iowa
City, Iowa, majored in physical educa-
tion. She holds a master's degree from
New York University and a doctorate
in psychology from the University of
Iowa. She was engaged in clinical psy-
chiatric work before joining the
WAVES.

1928

A son, John Charles, was born on February
8 to Mr. and Mrs. Ralph Butt (Marjorie Beard).
Marjorie was with the Grenfell Association in
Labrador for five years as principal of a school
in Northwest River. Mr. Butt is an agent of the
Hudson's Bay Company. They have spent the
past two years at Davis Inlet, Labrador. Marjorie has been with her father, Willard L. Beard,
'91, at Century Farm, Shelton, Connecticut,
since September, '42, but she and her husband and son will be somewhere in Canada soon.

1928 Continued

A full page portrait of the charming Mrs. John E. Rodgers as the "Bride of the Week" was published in the rotogravure section of the St. Louis Post Dispatch on March 14. Mrs. Rodgers, the former Miss Mary Ann Sargent of St. Louis, and Lieutenant John E. Rodgers were married on March 6. They are now living in Walla Walla, Washington, where Lt. Rodgers is a classifications officer at an Army Air Base.

Mrs. Ruth Tracy Millard has recently had a story entitled "I Go to Work by Moonlight," accepted for publication by The Saturday Evening Post.

Wallace Baldinger—See class of 1932.

1930

James Grant received his master's degree in the science of social administration at Western Reserve University on February 4.

1931

Mr. and Mrs. Kenneth W. Fraser (Emma Kathryn Ruch) are the parents of a daughter, Kathryn Louise, born May 5, 1942.

A letter from Sidney Bunker, '25, written from Ceylon in October, 1942, refers to the marriage of Eva Peek in July, to a British Naval Officer, John Grainger. Mrs. Grainger was on the staff of the school at Vaddukoddai, Ceylon. On her way there at the outbreak of the war, she had a perilous journey, including arrival in Honolulu Harbor at 8:00 a. m. of December 7, when the Japanese attacked.

Dr. and Mrs. Frederick R. White are the parents of a daughter, Anne Randolph, born January 8. Fred received his Ph.D. from the University of Michigan last June.

1932

The marriage of Lillian E. Alexander to Private Richard Ford Kinney took place on March 5 in Boston, Massachusetts.

Pvt. Robert D. Henry is listed in a government news release as one of the members of the armed forces who is a naturalized citizen. Bob

OBERLINITES AT NEWPORT TRAINING STATION
... editor of the station's newspaper is Chaplain Wolf

is a native of Ireland. He reported on April 17 at the Anti-aircraft Officer Candidate School, Camp Davis, North Carolina.

Mrs. Cullen B. Owens (Janet Russell, Con.) writes from Ithaca, New York, where her husband is an instructor of speech at Cornell University. They have a two year old son, Conrad.

Paul Anthony, Con., still lives in Cedar Rapids, Iowa, where he has been teaching school for the past eight years.

Wallace, '28, and Ellen Nichols Baldinger have a second child, Marna Louise, born August 6, 1942. They are still at Appleton, Wisconsin. Wallace is a professor of fine arts at Lawrence College.

1933

The Reverend and Mrs. George S. Howe announce the birth of a daughter, Nancy Georita, on January 28. Mr. Howe, who was formerly at Portlandville, New York, is now pastor of the Bethany Methodist Church at Bethany, Pennsylvania.

Lieutenant Talbot Harding and Miss Cecelia Mary Randall, of Worcester, England, were mar-

Pictured in the offices of Chaplain John D. Wolf, '39, at the U. S. Naval Training Station, Newport, Rhode Island, are, left to right: Chaplain Wolf, editor of the station newspaper, The Recruit, Store Keeper (1c) Dean H. Kelsey, '34, and Musician (1c) Edwin E. R. Heilakka, x'42.

ried on April 3 in the Church of SS. Philip and James in Hollow, Worcestershire, England. Lt. Harding is the son of Mr. '04, and Mrs. Richard T. F. Harding (Della Purcell, '03) of Cleveland. His wife is the daughter of Mr. and Mrs. J. W. C. Randall of Worcester. Her uncle, the Rev. Percival Warren, vicar of Tardebigge, performed the wedding ceremony. The couple are spending their honeymoon in the Cotswold Hills. Lt. Harding has been in England since December. He received his commission in the infantry at Officers' Candidate School at Ft. Benning, Georgia. Mrs. Harding is a graduate of St. Margaret's at Oxford and for three years taught in the schools in British Columbia.

A new address for Mrs. Thomas Y. McPherson (Marion Conant) is % Mrs. Nord, 6026 S. Kenwood, Chicago, Illinois. She is studying social service administration at the University of Chicago, having just been awarded the Edith Abbott Fellowship.

1934

Mr. and Mrs. William F. Tucker (Charlotte Macartney) are the parents of a son, Robert Morton, born on November 29, 1942. The Tucker family lives at 5230-57th So., Seattle, Washington.

Gretchen Hoornstra has been appointed women's personnel director of the Permold Company, Medina, Ohio, a war industry. Formerly a teacher at Cleveland's West High, a personnel worker for WPA, and recently a technician for the Graphite Bronze Company, she has had specialized training at Kent State University and in the Army Ordnance classes at Case School of Applied Science.

Mark Benjamin Willard was born on February 18 to Dr. and Mrs. John Willard (Adelaide Ela), 5427 Greenwood Avenue, Chicago.

1935

Josephine Hamilton, Con., and Herbert Van Meter, '37, were married on March 20 at the home of Jo's parents. Mr. and Mrs. Ralph O. Hamilton, 105 Franklin St., Greenfield, Massachusetts. Dean Graham performed the ceremony, assisted by Dr. George A. Martin, formerly of Springfield. Music at the wedding was provided by Mrs. Andrew Toussaint (Eleanor Clark, Con.) and Mrs. Max Ervin (Jane Burt, Con. '40). Also present were Charlotte Tinker, '37, Marion Beckwith, and Max Ervin, Con. '40.

The above report of the wedding was sent in by Mrs. Andrew G. Toussaint (Eleanor Clark, Con.) who reports that she has a son, Barry Clark, born August 14, 1942. Her husband

ON DUTY AT PATTERSON FIELD, DAYTON
... left to right, Lieutenant Anthony F. Piraino, '34; Lieutenant Ronald D. Rogers, '37, and T. Sgt. John F. Wright, Jr., x'44

works for Westinghouse in East Springfield, Massachusetts. and Eleanor plays the organ at her church. Her home address is 26 Elm St., Agawam, Mass.

A letter from Mrs. Milton E. Loomis (Ara Scotham, '11) reports that her daughter, Mrs. Charles R. Noback (Eleanor Loomis), is living at 1440 Highland Ave., Augusta, Georgia. Dr. Noback, her husband, is teaching in the Medical School of the University of Georgia. Her son, Charles Victor, is now twenty-one months. Her mother says that she is making a trip home, to Rochester, New York, soon.

Mr. and Mrs. Alfred Puhan (Fairfax Judd, '37) are enjoying life in New York City again where Al is employed by the Office of War Information. He started with OWI in May of 1942, but did not resign from the Rutgers University faculty until summer to spend full time at the new and "fascinating" work in New York.

1936

The marriage of Nuala Frost to Lieutenant Rankin Johnson, Jr., U. S. N. R., took place on February 27 in Santiago, Chile. Mrs. Johnson is the daughter of Wesley Frost, '07, United States Minister to Paraguay, and Mrs. Frost (Priscilla Clapp, '07). The couple are residing in Santiago, where Lieutenant Johnson is assistant naval attaché at the American Embassy.

C. Leland Barlow, Sp. 1/c W is on leave from the Oberlin Conservatory of Music faculty, stationed at Great Lakes Naval Training Station. He rehearses the Great Lakes Choir, famous for its weekly coast-to-coast radio broadcasts, has charge of the music at three church services each Sunday, gives voice tryouts for the new choir recruits and helps with informal "sing-song" sessions throughout the camp.

David H. Pinkney has been in London since January with one of the official missions attached to the U. S. Embassy.

Brenda B. Boynton, x, has been promoted to the rank of First Officer in the Women's Army Auxiliary Corps. This rank is equivalent to that of Captain in the Army. Brenda is now Director of the Physical Training Department at the Fort Des Moines Training Center.

1937

Frances Unkefer has taken a new position as executive secretary of the Jackson Branch of the Michigan Children's Aid Society. Her address is 612 First Street, Jackson, Michigan. Besides the regular children's case work, Fran's program will include the establishment of a boarding home.

Virginia Deringer Thompson (Mrs. Arthur T.) moved her cooperative house to the Delta Upsilon fraternity house when the Army Air Corps took over many of the women's dormitories at Syracuse University. Virginia reports seeing Dr. Perry Ayres, '38, Peg Stimson, '38, and Bob Vogel, '39, occasionally in Syracuse.

Herbert Van Meter—See class of 1935.

Walter Richards—See class of 1910.

Mrs. Fairfax Judd Puhan—See class of 1935.

1938

June Finnegan, x, has left her position with the Bell Telephone Company in Youngstown, Ohio, to join the WAVES. She is now in training at the Midshipman School, Northrop House, Northampton, Massachusetts.

Sherwood R. Moran, Jr., received his commission as an Ensign in the Naval Reserves in January and is now stationed abroad. Before leaving he brought his wife Frances Harvey Moran and their daughter Susan to Lima, Ohio, where they will stay for the duration.

1939

Dot Jones and Carl Schneider were married last summer. They are living in Madison, Wisconsin, where Carl is working on his doctoral thesis at the University of Wisconsin.

The wedding of Anna Catherine Davies and Dr. Wade Volwiler took place on March 13 in the Presbyterian Church of Ben Avon, Pennsylvania, followed by a reception at the home of the bride's parents. Dr. and Mrs. Volwiler will live in Brookline, Massachusetts. Dr. Volwiler, who was graduated with honors from Harvard Medical School on March 10, will intern at Massachusetts General Hospital in Boston.

Lieutenant, '41, and Mrs. Thomas C. Dutton (Elizabeth Tuckerman) announce the birth of a daughter, Jean Marcia, April 12, in Cleveland. Tom is with the Marine Corps, somewhere in the Pacific.

Eugene M. Farber and John J. Gerling were awarded degrees of doctor of medicine at the University of Buffalo, March 24.

1940

The engagement of Jessie Isaacs to Daniel Warren Boxwell, of Peabody, Massachusetts, has been announced by Dr., '11, and Mrs. L. M. Isaacs (Helen French, x'14). Mr. Boxwell was graduated from Bowdoin College in '38 and is now studying at Chicago Theological Seminary.

A card from S. Lua Syckes reports that on March 20 he received his Navigators Wings and commission as a second lieutenant in the Air Corps. He has been appointed an instructor and will teach navigation in the advanced school at Monroe, Louisiana.

Esther Gott—See class of 1909.

Sgt. John K. Bare is serving in the Adjutant General Section of Tenth Corps Headquarters, U. S. Army, in Sherman, Texas. He was a graduate assistant in psychology at Brown University before his induction last July.

Daniel A. Kyser writes, "seeing my name 'Private' in the Alumni Magazine, also with all my changes in address in the past, I figure I had better inform the College of my status at present.

"I am now in charge of Artillery Band in Camp Van Dorn, Mississippi. I have been, for the past two and one-half months, in Washington, D. C., taking training for Band Leader at the Army Music School. The school graduated, on January 16, 75 Warrant Officers, Junior Grade, all of whom have gone out as band leaders to the different camps and divisions all over the U. S. Although I haven't had the band very long here, I find it very interesting work, very fine for the men, for a band is a 'morale builder' in the army.

"Hope everything is going along fine at Oberlin. I sure would like to be there and look around for a few days. I imagine quite a few changes have been made since I was there."

OBERLIN GET-TOGETHER AT FORT McCLELLAN
... graced by the presence of Corporal Saint's bride.

WHEN OBERLIN alumni stationed with units at Fort McClellan, Alabama, got together in March for a session of reminiscences at one of the Fort chapels, the meeting was graced by the presence of the bride of one of the men, herself an Oberlin graduate. The newlyweds were Corporal William Saint, '42, of Erie, Pennsylvania, and Mrs. Saint, the former Barbara Booth, '42, of Binghamton, New York.

Others in the group were Captain Andrew L. Johnson, '38, Chaplain of the 92nd Infantry Division; Lieutenant Robert B. Powell, '26, chaplain of the 1st Regiment of Fort McClellan's Infantry Replacement Training Center; Corporal Charles B. Woodbury, '40, of Washington, D. C.; and Corporal Monroe Bond, x'44, of Lorain, Ohio. The group was brought together by Chaplain Powell, and is shown in front of the altar of his chapel.

Front row, left to right: Captain Johnson, Lieutenant Powell; back row, left to right: Corporal Saint, Mrs. Saint, Corporal Bond and Corporal Woodbury.

1941

Zeno Wicks has been awarded a graduate Eastman Kodak Company fellowship at the University of Illinois in chemistry for the 1943-44 school year.

Mr., x, and Mrs. William D. Swetland, Jr., of New York City, announce the birth of a son, William D., III, on March 21.

ENSIGN JIM ARNOLD, '42
... *commissioned an Ensign at the U. S. Naval Air Training Center, Corpus Christi, Texas, on April 7, James T. Arnold, '42, has an assignment as flying instructor. His specialty training was with torpedo planes.*

Mr. and Mrs. George Vradenburg (Beatrice White, x'44) are the parents of a son, George Albert, born on March 14. George is at the New River, North Carolina, Marine base.

Lieutenant Thomas C. Dutton—See class of 1939.

Bob Beers' engagement to Evelyn Gracey, '43, was announced recently.

1942

The marriage of Eleanor Hewins to "Larry" Smith took place February 27 in Sikeston, Missouri. Larry is an aviation cadet in the Army Air Corps.

The engagement of Caroline Penfield Atwater to Lieutenant Edwin Slater Leonard, son of Dr. and Mrs. Harold J. Leonard (Marian Slater, '11) has been announced. Lieutenant Leonard, who attended Columbia College before entering the Army Signal Corps, is now on duty overseas. Caroline is the great-granddaughter of the Rev. Thornton Bigelow Penfield, '56; Lieutenant Leonard is a grandson of Mrs. Edwin S. Slater (Sarah L. Greer, '84) and the late Mr. Slater, '83.

Mildred Woodard has been a librarian at the General Radio Company in Cambridge, Massachusetts, since January.

The engagement of Elizabeth Moore to Ronald Vingoe. of Dayton, Ohio, has been announced. Elizabeth is doing secretarial work at the War Production Board in Cleveland. Her fiance, who is a graduate of the College of Engineering and Commerce at the University of Cincinnati, is associated with the War Department at Wright Field, Dayton, as a chemical engineer.

Frances Osborn, x, was married to Victor Larsen, U. S. N. R., on January 30 in Bethesda, Maryland.

When Don Emig was in Oberlin recently on vacation from Yale Divinity School, he became engaged to Betty John, '43.

Gertrude (Trudie) Colson and Private Howard Nicholson were married December 20, 1942, in Calvary Cathedral, Sioux Falls, South Dakota. Mrs. Lee Girton (Alice Boyce, Con. '05-'06) was a witness at the wedding. Mr. and Mrs. Nicholson were in Oberlin from March 23 to 27 on a "delayed honeymoon." Howard is stationed at Sioux Falls.

Helen Humbert, '43, and Ensign John Bartow were married March 27 in the Marble Collegiate Church, Fifth Ave., New York City. John is the son of Mrs. G. E. Bartow (Desdemona Borthwick. '05). Helen Bartow is back in school.

Ruth Gott—See class of 1909.

J. R. King, Jr., is conductor of the Berea College band. During a recent program of Music of the United Nations, his organization introduced the Berea Pep Song. written by Mr. King and George R. Bent, '20.

1944

Naomi Rickert, x, is now Mrs. Russell J. Minott. Her husband, from Greenfield, Massachusetts, is a ski trooper stationed at Camp Hale in the Rockies. Mrs. Minott is living at Mt. Hermon, Massachusetts, where she has been a secretary on the staff of Mount Hermon School.

First Tabulations in 1943 Alumni Fund

CLASS RECORDS AS OF APRIL 10

Class	No. in Class	Quota 1943	Contributed to Date	Amount Contributed 1942
Prior to 1891	314	$ 571.10	$ 111.00	$ 508.50
1891	45	122.78	120.00	177.00
1892	34	98.95	14.00	121.20
1893	53	173.53	7.00	294.60
1894	72	261.93	28.00	316.50
1895	36	144.00	10.00	85.50
1896	54	235.74	202.00	368.40
1897	59	257.55	38.00	290.15
1898	63	275.00	666.00	457.50
1899	86	375.44	315.00	1,387.00
1900	70	309.59	197.00	356.00
1901	57	248.83	19.00	818.50
1902	65	283.75		296.50
1903	91	397.26	39.50	500.50
1904	78	340.50	42.50	1,532.50
1905	102	445.29	33.50	224.00
1906	119	519.50	40.50	547.00
1907	133	580.60	56.00	264.00
1908	127	554.40	26.00	374.50
1909	121	528.20	34.00	546.50
1910	169	737.75	77.50	851.00
1911	168	733.40	39.00	527.00
1912	184	803.25	60.00	356.50
1913	197	860.00	64.00	532.50
1914	181	790.15	53.00	532.00
1915	193	842.55	46.50	763.00
1916	194	811.60	41.00	340.50
1917	199	774.60	103.00	686.50
1918	229	849.75	70.00	410.50
1919	174	633.00	34.00	322.00
1920	222	759.15	27.00	274.00
1921	226	707.00	65.00	468.40
1922	233	678.10	35.00	272.00
1923	268	740.95	27.00	224.50
1924	268	701.95	26.00	253.29
1925	278	687.70	36.25	224.50
1926	265	617.00	196.50	232.00
1927	303	661.35	80.25	181.50
1928	353	719.15	152.00	444.00
1929	286	540.90	29.50	165.50
1930	297	518.63	77.50	146.38
1931	323	517.00	87.00	263.16
1932	310	465.65	63.50	210.50
1933	276	361.45	58.00	261.24
1934	322	386.55	57.50	215.50
1935	242	193.65	59.00	113.75
1936	300	218.28	82.00	180.00
1937	312	204.30	82.00	173.75
1938	329	191.50	73.00	207.25
1939	347	176.75	82.00	198.50
1940	341	148.86	73.50	159.00
1941	351	127.69	91.00	228.23
1942	320	116.41	80.00	
Friends and Former Students			336.00	1,337.18
Totals	10,439	$25,000.00	$ 4,436.50	$21,241.48

Letters . . .

(Continued from Inside Front Cover)

Sgt. Garrison Looks Upon Oberlin With Vicarious Pride

March 15, 1943

Dear Mr. Wilkins:

It is heartening, and characteristic, that Oberlin should be thinking and planning concretely for the PEACE, even when the war is at flood tide. Those of us who are prohibited from making public statements may take a vicarious pride from those of you who may speak out as you please about any problem that you please. Make it strong, make it courageous, and above all else, make such plans as will bed down idealism with realities. The two are not incompatible, cynics to the contrary; the union, however, is difficult, to put it mildly.

In such discussions, the idealists are apt to smell the heady bouquet of the brave new world, and tumble head-first into generalizations about the obvious brotherhood of man, the urge of people for peace, the immediate feasibility of the parliament of man and the federation of the world. (My Tennyson has rusted a little!) Idealists—especially young ones!—fail to grasp the fact that nothing is solid gain except that which comes from evolution: grinding, slow, painful growth. Consequently, they expect the world to turn in horror from the carnage just past; to begin a new way, untried but hopeful, toward mankind's liberation. Their plans sound wonderful. All of our desperate hopes seem fulfilled. THE PLAN is reasonable because it touches the goodness in all of us, it fans the inner hope we have that man is really good and well-meaning.

Yet of all the theorists, the unbridled idealist is the most dangerous. He gives a picture of man's estate so cleanly invigorating in its scope, that we cannot help taking it in. We want it that way so urgently, that we believe it immediately possible. And when, as inevitably it must, the dream tarnishes and the sweet hope grows old with waiting, both the idealist and those he persuaded are apt to swing bitterly to pessimism and disillusioned inaction. Or else, as Wilson did, they break their hearts against a monumental inertia which has killed such men time out of mind.

On the other hand, the so-called realists, bent upon proving that man is a social aggregate of venality and self-interest, swings so far to the other extreme that he damns all hopes, curses the past, despairs of the future, and binds himself inexorably to the present. In doing so, he loses the faith of those who might have followed him or his ideas. The realist's method of immoral expediency he justifies by immediate results; long-term benefits do not concern him. He lives for today, and his tomorrow brings the taste of ashes.

Yet, what is the middle course? I wish I knew. It must be hard, because if it were easy, it would be wrong. Perhaps it lies in the realm of ordinary things, a million times expanded: decency, stretched from man to man out to nations and their neighbors—decency that involves effort and sacrifice and well-considered legislation; the necessity of laws backed by force, expanded from community scope to world scope.

What is decent government but the existence of laws, mutually agreed upon and firmly enforced? We can legislate the laws, but we must enforce their intent. The enforcement—aye, there's the rub—for there the ideal must lower itself to the extent of getting tough. If we can do that, then we will be on our way toward a better world.

(St. Sgt.) ROGER H. GARRISON, '40

Former Noah-Gables Boy Wins Navigator's Wings

A letter written to Mrs. Spartoco Di Biasio (Antoinette Zanolli) class correspondent for 1940.

Selman Field, Louisiana.

Dear Tony:

Remember me? Just one of those lucky Noah boys that was honored at eating with all you beautiful girls at Gables—some three years back.

This is all beating around the bush though, as my main purpose in writing you is to give you some info: Last week I finally finished my cadet training and received my commission and navigator's wings in the Air Corps. Of our class of 250 10 were retained as instructors, and somehow or other I managed to be one of them; so I guess I'll be pounding navigation into the cadets brains for several months to come. At present I'm attending the school for instructors here on the post, where we get a lot of that valuable (?) lesson planning and education psych. stuff. This lasts for three weeks and then I start giving it out myself.

When at Maxwell Field last summer I saw Captain Raymond Fisher (formerly of the Oberlin faculty) and had quite a long talk with him about Oberlin. Here in Monroe I have seen Jerry Schloerb, '42, and Louise Pinger, '39. Both are married, Jerry to a lieutenant on the field here. There probably are some other Oberlin fellows around, but I haven't met any as yet.

Keep 'em smiling!

—S. Lua Syckes, '40·
2nd Lt. A. C.

P. S.:

I have run into a couple of navigators, now stationed here, who were with John Steinbinder, '40· in the Pacific area. They praised his work highly. (They are Cpt. Schneider, Cpt. Roberts and Lt. Brown.)

Navy Sends Him to Harvard in Winter, New Orleans for Summer

March 13, 1943

Dear Tom:

As I recall the proper way to begin a letter such as this is to say, "I do appreciate your sending me a copy of the Oberlin Alumni Magazine." And since that is exactly how I reacted when I received it please consider my appreciation as being expressed.

For the last five months I have been stationed at Harvard while the Navy has tried to make a communicator out of me. Now that this course has been completed it so happens that the powers that be have decided that I need some more education. Hence I have been ordered to report for further instruction for a period of what looks like about five more months to another school. However, Oberlin need not turn crimson

with shame as there were about twenty-five more who received the same orders. I am really very pleased with these new orders for if all goes well I should have a fair chance of getting something rather nice at the end of the training. At least I will be getting in some sea duty during the next few months.

Our company is made up of men from every state. The truth is that we give Oberlin a fairly good bit of competition when the subject of states represented comes up. However, the South seems to be the best represented. These boys certainly are living examples of "State's Rights." Really they almost have me believing that the real purpose of the Civil War was to determine how great was the desire of the North to remain annexed to the South. Now that is not true as any Oberlinite will agree. The real purpose was to test the ability of the last station of the underground railway to maintain its line of communication. Although I find that the Texans will pipe down when asked concerning the election of one Pappy O'Daniels the boys from North Carolina are beyond all hope of redemption.

Although I am an outcast of the USO I can say that I have found the people whom I have met in Boston and Cambridge to be most hospitable. They certainly are doing their best to make all the men here realize that those who aren't in uniform are solidly behind the war effort.

When you write to Bob Cornelius please extend to him my regards. I know what he means when he says that he'd like more action. You might remind him that it's a long climb from the double bottom of a battleship to topside when things have to be jettisoned. After all New Orleans should be very decent at this time of year. As a matter of fact I hope to be in New Orleans for the summer season. That shows how little change there is in one's life, even in the navy. You see I continue to do things as no other person would do them—Boston for the winter, the South for the summer.

President Wilkins recently wrote to me here. That man really is doing a marvelous piece of work. I do not understand how he is able to carry on this self-imposed obligation of writing to Oberlin men in the service. That in itself should be a full time job. He really deserves all honor and credit for this activity.

Here's another name for the long list of Oberlin men in uniform. Heiser, M. F., Class '34· He is an Ensign U. S. N. R. At the present he is living in 17 Weld Hall, constructed about 1778. I do not know for how long he will be here. However, I have the impression that he will not be transferred until about July. Any mail addressed to him at N. T. S. Harvard (Communications) will eventually reach him.

Keep up the good work, Tom. More than ever are we needing institutions such as Oberlin.

BOB BOLBACH, '33

Dear Sirs:

Just received my copy of the Oberlin Alumni Magazine, in newspaper form. Let me convey my thanks, and assure you it was indeed welcome; and a pleasure to read about old friends and classmates. Hope you continue the paper. It's great!

Yours sincerely,

Pvt. James White, X'37.

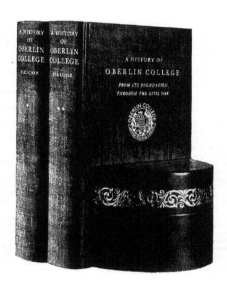